MASS MEDIA,
EDUCATION,
AND A
BETTER SOCIETY

JAY W. STEIN

NELSON-HALL ⊞ CHICAGO

To the parents, teachers, students, communicators, and civic leaders who interpret and practice education as enlightenment and who believe that its spirit in a democracy has no bounds.
And to children, young people, and fellow citizens, and to their teachers in all their variety everywhere throughout life.

Library of Congress Cataloging in Publication Data

Stein, Jay Wobith, 1920-
  Mass media, education, and a better society.

  Bibliography: p.
  Includes index.
  1. Mass media—Social aspects—United States.
2.   Education—United States. I. Title.
HN90.M3S73   301.16'1   79-11517
ISBN 0-88229-310-9

Manufactured in the United States of America

10   9   8   7   6   5   4   3   2   1

CONTENTS

FOREWORD

When ancient Egyptians began to write on papyrus rather than on stone, communication became portable. A king's power could extend over more area than ever before, but his expanded authority had to encompass the scribes and the papyrus-makers. As Erik Barnouw, a noted historian of communications, said: "Papyrus begat bureaucracy." The dissemination of edicts required a delegation of authority which, in turn, led to an increasingly complex structure in society.

The printing press with moveable type brought books to the people. Knowledge could no longer belong exclusively to those with political power or high socioeconomic status. The technological change in communications advanced social change toward democracy, as the common man became more able to share experiences and feelings with others. The ancient Greeks had believed that democratic participation was limited to the number of people who could assemble in an arena at one time to hear their political candidates speak. The printing press gradually expanded that number to all those who could read what the candidates had to say. Later the camera and the telephone transmitted images and sounds more authentically than ever thought possible and reached even larger masses of people.

Radio made news events immediate and often heart-wrenchingly close. To anyone who has heard the taped voice of the reporter at the Hindenburg disaster, the experience is almost as real as when it happened. Our memories are formed by that one perception; we are joined in the same frame of reference. Franklin D. Roosevelt was a "radio" president. He knew how to reach the people in a very personal way with his fireside chats. He brought Americans closer to the days of the Greek arena, to the shared, immediate view.

And then came television. John F. Kennedy felt that television won him the presidency. Richard M. Nixon agreed with him about television's impact recalling how television enabled him to make the Checkers speech that saved his vice-presidential campaign. Each president has used television more than his predecessor, bringing the chief executive that much closer to the people. The use of debate in the last election showed that television affects the outcome, but it need not determine it. By becoming a fixture in elections to come, television debates in a sense will help to bring us full circle back to the Greek arena.

Americans spend more time watching television than in any other activity except sleeping. The New York State Assembly acknowledged television's importance by voting it among the basic necessities that may not be touched by creditors. Television brings us together as we mourn the death of a president, exult over a trip to the moon, or hold our breath during negotiations with a terrorist. We live in a neighborhood where Archie Bunker, Mary Tyler Moore, and Walter Cronkite are prominent citizens. But television separates us too as we sit, arranged like spokes of a wheel, facing the set at the hub, because it is easier to watch together than to talk together. In fact, we barely watch; we absorb. Television has changed our perceptions even more dramatically than the printing press changed the perceptions of our ancestors.

Educators have largely ignored the impact of the media, even fought against it. Could it be that when books were first mass-produced, teachers resisted them, fearing the death of the oral tradition? Some educators have regarded television as a threat to the use of books and to the personal contact between student and teacher. They do not see that television transmission of educational content can free the teacher to have more contact with his students. They do not note that books like *The Ascent of Man, The Forsythe Saga,* and *The Adams Chronicles* appeared on best-seller lists after the series were on the air.

Fortunately, the educational capabilities of the media for the millions have been rapidly surfacing in recent years. Millions of children have learned fundamentals of elementary education through a variety of early morning television programs, sections of their daily newspaper, and selected comic magazines. A critical situation was alleviated in the winter of 1977, when numerous schools were closed due to severe cold, because newspapers printed homework assignments and television stations allowed teachers to present class-time instruction so that students would not fall behind.

Former Federal Communications Commissioner Nicholas Johnson said that all television is educational. The same may be said of the other media. People must ask themselves, then, what they are learning from the media. And if they are not satisfied with the answer, educators must take a much more active role.

In this book, Professor Stein discusses the conflict between the mass media for the millions and public education. His rationale of the pressing need for better cooperation and understanding between them is sound and his call for action involves them both. All of those who work in education or in the media, as well as those who think of their own schooling, read newspapers, watch television, or are part of other media audiences, will do well to read on.

NELL MINOW
Chicago, Illinois

America's foremost developmental task is to provide the world with the leadership of a republic of citizens broadly enough educated to build a better civilization. For more than a generation our educational system has outdone itself in building citizen technocrats and nearly undone itself in failing to educate for citizenship. We live at a time which is forcing us to come to grips with this apparent polarization.

It is correct to insist that our mass trade education is insufficient. Both as a long-time executive in the newspaper medium and as a participant in all of the mass media, I have come to see a critical lack grow more acute. Skilled mechanics, engineers, lawyers, doctors, and educators are able to find individual pigeon holes for themselves in our miraculously effective economic system. But the system does precious little to educate them as citizens who can vote in the most intelligent manner on significant issues. It does not orient them in improving the system, either socially or economically.

The vehicles having the capacity to turn our skillful tradesmen into skillful builders of civilization largely operate apart from organized education. It is public mass communications that make the voter knowledgeable and motivate him to participate in and enrich his democracy to the extent that he does so. The essential problem to which this book addresses itself is the magnitude of overcommunication versus the under-utilization of the media toward constructive ends.

In contrast to most of the world, America has more communication media than it can effectively use. We are inundated with sights and sounds. Resultant problems inhibit the task of American leadership. In this book, the author suggests the rerouting of this near calamitous over-communicating and points to the immediate and imperative need for better direction without delay. Such movements as adult or continuing education, or educational alternatives, or Common Cause touch the surface, but they remain hidebound so long as they do not face the effect and the potential of the public mass media.

Already some public mass communication is so entertaining, so inspiring, and so educational that it has taken some of its audience beyond formal education in both breadth and depth. In a mass-media world, it is not unrealistic to conceive of an entire people becoming knowledgeable, possessing economic wisdom and a sense of lasting social justice for a world with less want and more hope for tomorrow.

Robert C. Dille
Carmel, California

PREFACE

When I was a boy of nine, I played in the boys' band of my small home town in the Midwest. The bandstand was a large parade wagon parked every Saturday night in the center of Main Street and adorned with strings of incandescent lights. The weekly concert stimulated the business of local merchants.

Hundreds (it seemed more like thousands) of people from the community and surrounding farms roamed the streets, munching popcorn and chattering about the news, the weather, and other varied concerns. Always they kept the band music in listening range. The twenty-three players were well rehearsed in their selections and crowded into the bandwagon itself, drawing large crowds.

Since that day, the bandwagon has become the depersonalized dominance and ubiquitous umbrella of television and the other mass media. The new bandwagon not only attracts, it also engulfs, for people more than ever desire it in their midst wherever they are, day or night. The revolution in electronics, engineering, and organization has helped people realize the desire for communications everywhere at all times. Nowadays everyone feels the drawing power of television, radio, the movies, recordings, newspapers, magazines, and paperbacks. These seven media are irresistible to the millions.

As the mass media have become today's bandwagon, people have let it magnetize and addict them during almost every activity—eating, drinking, driving, sleeping, worshipping, politicking, and even dying. In all its forms, the band plays on, but now none of the players knows the identities of the invisible millions in the audiences, nor do the millions know the players except as replication of image and sound, ink and paper.

As a parent, a teacher, a citizen, and one concerned with being a social person, I feel intense anxiety. A relatively small number of people commiserate with me. Together we few dread the thought of being made to act against our wills. We observe children and students and teachers and fellow citizens pulled along in directions which separate them from us and from each other, hypnotized and changed into something they neither intend nor wish to be. So thoroughly do they lose their individual dignity that they are no longer aware of the loss.

The place which we (my wife and I and our five children) call home has no "bandwagons"—well, almost none! There are a few shelves of worthy paperbacks, hundreds of fine, hardback books, a local newspaper, a radio which is tuned for news and weather, and a record player for fine tunes. A choice magazine or two, like *National Geographic*, receives the same kind of attention as attendance at a quality movie seen two or three times a year. The comic magazines meet code standards and the television viewing is selective.

Why? The answer is simply that we prize our personal freedom. It is a way of expressing distaste for mindless acceleration, exaggeration and distortion, which massacres precious hours and people. We want relief from the twisting, shouting, barking, pummeling mania that threatens both mental and physical health.

By largely turning my back on the media, I can realize the reason and integrity that are bred only in an environment permitting calm and concentration. Hence, I can peer out of my isolation, exit and reenter at will, and mingle in the world of human relationships. I can enjoy myriad attractive pursuits and endeavors, such as music, sports, reading mysteries, and the beauty of nature. A preference for the hermitage is a return to reason and responsibility.

At the heart of the hermitage is education—liberal and general in content—with characteristic excellence and endurance. Once constructed, this life style cannot be antagonistic toward the mass media. Inescapable outside, the seven media now come inside. Their forces and configurations pass through a screening process, a framework that sorts and conditions.

Through an educated mind I can see them all—the unfortunate inputs as well as the beneficial gems. The mass communicators no longer obscure from me the ability to make wise choices among infinite alternatives. I can maintain my reason and sanity, my objectivity, my peace of mind, and can make order out of the incessant exposures and injections. I am no longer a nonentity among countless millions dependent upon modern band-wagons. I am an individual human being in command of self, with spirit and dignity. I see other individuals as real, live human beings in need of interpersonal, warm communication. Most important, the educated mind gives me the ability to recognize the many excellent qualities of media content. I give thanks for what the media do accomplish. I set about, as an educator, a parent, a student and a citizen, to help make the media accomplish all of the benefits they can and should, to identify and support the human perspectives and purposes. It is this kind of endeavor which underlay the making of a book entitled *Mass Media, Education and a Better Society*. I hope you agree with me that the media are too important to separate from formal education at any level.

Jay W. Stein
Macomb, Illinois

1

NIGHTMARE
AND
FETISH

Next year, a decade or more from now, or in the year 2079—select whatever date you wish, you can hear or read about someone who has proclaimed with conviction that the outlook for human survival beyond a certain date is dismal. Insecurity. Inflation. Overpopulation. Unemployment. Hunger. Disease. Addiction. Campus turbulence. Citizen apathy and disgust. Hate. Demonstrations. Corruption. Violence. Crime. Assassination. War. The crass misery of social problems converges and descends like a nightmare. Studying the situation in the 1970s, writers and speakers warn that it invites apprehension and portends annihilation.

Common are social science textbook titles with words such as "problems," "crisis," or "pathology," words that reflect a troublesome state of affairs. The topics covered include mass terror, thermonuclear war, genocide, and alienation. One typical preface reads: "Civilization may be *in extremis*; human sensibility is under fire; we are threatened on every side. At such a time, he who remains in his accustomed groove could indeed find that it will be his grave."[1] A Harvard University biologist confesses: "I am one of those scientists who does not see how to bring the human race much past the year 2000." His plea: "Arise, ye prisoners of extinction."[2]

The public mass media are a convenient scapego͏͏ ͏ the disturbing confusion that surrounds the crises. Very few peop͏ ͏nd it. Few analyze, as this book does, how the media are a f͏ ͏ssive, pulverizing magic and in the illumination of hu͏ ͏ ͏a are massive; they are potentially of terrifying, treme͏.

Much of the same analysis may be made of the second major social force and convenient scapegoat, namely public education. The two forces lie at the base of a critical dilemma of civilization.

The turmoil of overcommunication confronts the tranquil prolongation of undereducation. Eventually the two forces either will cancel each other out or they will join hands. The outlook for a merging of the public media and education, as the real dilemma is analyzed and resolved by cooperative action, can become one of hope and conviction.

It is the second force, education, that people have traditionally shaped to answer their fears and uncertainties. Americans feel that the freedom and responsibility to learn and to teach are fundamental in their heritage. They study language, literature, philosophy, and government. They develop the skills of reading, writing, and calculating. From a rich and varied heritage, they cultivate a breadth and depth of human wisdom. By exploring a wide range of moral, social, and intellectual values, Americans are able to identify and claim the highest possible ideals. They can commend themselves for their many educational achievements, particularly for the high schools and colleges of liberal arts and general studies, to which have been entrusted the tasks of creating answers and finding pragmatic solutions.

Then someone punctures the pride and hope by asking, "But how many finish high school? How many attend college?" And Americans realize that the question might well be "How few are we?" The fact is that in any one year those who are affiliated with a college or university as either a learner or teacher are only a small fraction of the nation's population.

The response to this inadequacy, education promoters say, is simple. People need merely build more and bigger schools and develop more classroom and laboratory facilities for teaching larger groups. They need new mechanical and electronic teaching aids to supplement the established procedures of assignments, study, lecture, recitation, and examination. Thus the campus can grow in size. More teachers, technicians, clerks and maintenance personnel will join the staffs of colleges and universities. The college becomes an even bigger business in the community. More students will enroll, and more will graduate. The machine will hum still more comfortingly. These are the requisites.

But a paradox exists. Each person defines and justifies his role in society in precise occupational terms, with little or no concern for genuine education. The typical educator is no exception. He organizes his profession and prescribes the steps and facilities for acquiring his particular offerings. He measures the progress of his learner-clients, and when they complete a course according to standards, he certifies them with academic credits and stamps each production unit with a degree. Despite the supposedly high value on education, people seldom question or care whether or not a learner actually has become liberally educated.

To an even smaller degree people query how other means necessary for becoming educated can be made available and usable. For years, economic realities have ruled education. Since most people must aim first at becoming income producers, a liberal-general education has a market priority lower than the services of an unskilled worker. Educational responsibility has been relegated to a professional segment of society, and people have widely believed it best to leave it there. With little or no interference, therefore, teachers and administrators have largely applied parochial minds to their task, and they have splintered university and college curricula almost irretrievably.

In the chapters that follow, these concerns of liberal-general educators and students are frankly and openly faced. The average high school graduate and college enrollee lack the spirit needed to enable them to desire or to utilize the enlightenment that comes through education. If these students have a modicum of honest interest or drive in this direction, they soon lose it, or they fight a severe battle to maintain it. The school and college years leave them with little or no insight into the secrets of educating oneself outside the classroom. The students have little or no disposition to exemplify and teach what they have learned or to dare to promote the principle of responsibility necessary for a healthy democracy.

By contrast, less tested principles have been most daringly espoused. Television, radio, movies, recordings, magazines, newspapers and paperback books persistently shout their messages. The mass media are everywhere with daily and hourly impact. People learn, think, act, laugh and cry with them. They are the most powerful agency ever devised for impressing values, facts and ideas on the minds of millions. Whereas the schools encounter some of the population for a fraction of the time, the mass media reach most of the population most of the time. The schools use the limited methods of a classroom setting; the mass media utilize every possible device for total sensory appeal.

For millions with taboos and indifference about education, the mass media deliver a revelry of mediocre content and indiscreet invitation. Under pressures of incessant repetition almost everywhere, even the college-bred persons compromise important principles of liberal learning. They may despise the intellectual level and cultural taste of the great majority, but they lack the understanding and concern that would help them to raise the common standards. Among those who profess to hate the media are many who accept and patronize what they know to be its cheap content. Civic leaders work to contain and eliminate physical slums, but they hesitate to discuss the intellectual and moral slums that surround human minds and push inexorably upon all people, respecting no bounds.

Among the indifferent and neglectful leaders, exceptions do exist. Spokesmen in the public communications industries—the president of a network, the director of a news syndicate—on occasion eloquently endorse high cultural and political values. Their producers and editors select for mass distribution impressive offerings that measure up to educational standards: the analysis of a political campaign, the pros and cons on such issues as pesticides or planned parenthood, visits to classical Greece, or perspectives on opera or art. A citizen can enroll in a televised "Sunrise Semester" or "Continental Classroom." He can subscribe to "Great Books"; he can join a classical recordings club. He can join millions in radio programs that comprise a veritable university of the air.

Some educators—the exceptions—openly acknowledge these efforts by the media and urge their use in the classroom. A few professors compile guides or conduct workshops related to using the media. The National Council of Teachers of English shows how to relate certain outstanding movies to the paperback edition of the books. The National Education Association and the National Council for the Social Studies have joined with the television networks in the preparation of study guides for the media as adventures in learning. Scattered courses survey the history and role of films in modern times. Where more comprehensive courses exist, they tend to be attached to departments of English or journalism or to new schools sometimes organized as panaceas for the world's problems. Under the aegis of various organizations, and with the aid of foundation or government grants, educators have published scholarly findings on the communication process and have engaged in stimulating controversies over freedom and censorship.

Although these endeavors are commendable, they may so far be characterized as minor in scope and weak in effect. Communicators have long taken a defensive stance toward education; educators, a suspicious tone toward the media. The competitive spirit between them dwells on means rather than ends. Any efforts at coordination lack the impetus for and promise of wide adaptation and full cooperation.

Despite gorgeously printed promotional booklets from the television networks and other media centers, few educators read them or see the cultural or civic programs they describe. An excellent column in the *NEA Reporter*, entitled "Current, What's Going On In TV, Radio, Press, Films, and National Magazines," is read for personal enjoyment, but one wonders whether it is used for the enrichment of classroom assignments. Among teachers, the term "mass media" denotes tailor-made audiovisual aids, teaching machines and other devices for expediting classroom instruction to larger groups. For some businessmen, the term refers only to advertising by a particular medium such as television or newspapers.

A general concept of a public communications system that simultaneously embraces broadcast, film and print media is seldom entertained by educators and little developed by communications spokesmen. The interest of the former is the classroom; of the latter, the particular medium that pays him. There the concern usually stops. One strains to find a serious study of the role of liberal-general education compared and contrasted to the role of public communications. One asks whether, in fact, both sides consider the prospects of genuine cooperation in responsible public service to be impractical and remote.

This book, then, is about the public campus (both high school and college) and public communications; it proposes a common venture of the two into liberal-general education for the entire population. It considers the claims of spokesmen for each side, the commentaries of scholars, and the frank remarks of critics. The message of the book comes from a citizen, parent and educator who believes that the great majority of individuals in a democratic nation desire enlightenment and that leaders are available to give it. To convey his message, the author analyzes problems arising from the differing revolutionary paces of the two leading channels of enlightenment—the campus and the media. He offers some ideas for resolution of the problems that separate these channels from each other.

Any book about American education can be a glorious description of accomplishments. They have been many, and they deserve much praise. The author has frequently expressed his own deep admiration for the American system of education, and he has devoted his life to service in its support and development. His comments in these chapters stem directly from his associations with and high regard for the dedicated and capable teachers and administrators in the schools and colleges of the United States and the several agencies of professional organization and counsel. Similarly he can note his numerous and satisfying associations with the mass media.

A book on the subject of education and communications might, in addition to the foregoing, describe the occasional use of mass media in the schools or the employment of educators in the mass media. It might correlate enrollment in college with elaborate statistics on reading, listening and viewing. It might be a survey of research on the media and the schools, an anthology of opinions about them, or a history of them. The author recognizes all of these purposes as worthwhile ventures and refers to several that have been attempted.

Esoteric writing about the mass media became the successful endeavor of Marshall McLuhan during the 1960s. He punned that "the medium is the message," i.e., the medium is more important in itself than what is transmitted, and "the medium is the massage," i.e., it roughs up and massages our senses, "altering the environment of our preelectronic world."[3] McLuhan described the media as "hot" or "cold" in proportion to the relative amount of information the media or the audience brought to the communication.

Response to McLuhan was mixed.[4] An Amherst College professor said: "He's swinging, switched on, with it, and NOW, and wrong." An English critic called his writing "deliberately antilogical, circular, repetitious, unqualified, gnomic, outrageous." Historian Arthur M. Schlesinger, Jr., stated: "One comes away with the feeling that here is an intelligent man who for reasons of his own prefers to masquerade as a charlatan." Schlesinger added: "It is not easy to do justice to the brilliant and chaotic combination of bland assertion, astute guesswork, fake analogy, dazzling insight, hopeless nonsense, shockmanship, showmanship, wisecracks and oracular mysticism which mingles so confidently and haphazardly in the circular McLuhan monologue."[4]

The critical need is for a sensible analysis, a meaningful framework, and a workable challenge for further thinking and possible action. Looking deeply into the social functions and comparative effects of education and communications, people need fearlessly to express what they see. They must not merely note and evaluate the dangers, but also must seek and appreciate the hopeful prospects. In a tragic shortsightedness, many social planners saw the dramatic increase during the 1960s of the college-age population as the signal for the permanent expansion of colleges and universities. They isolated such expansion from the role of the mass media in the distribution of education. Attention to the Federal Communications Commission or to other government operations relative to the mass communication of ideas might well have prevented the impending campus problems surrounding expansion. Indeed, it took only a few years of decreasing school and college enrollments to warn educators away from the expansion programs.

The disillusionment and schizophrenia suffered by students and other citizens, the differential in pace and coverage between the revolution that is campus education and the revolution that is public communications, the common bond of learning and teaching in the classroom and through the mass media are all interrelated subjects that merit discussion here. Their treatment in this book carries no pretense to novelty or finality. This book stresses and elaborates upon an untapped potential—the media—that could and should be widely used in the liberal and general education of the general public in which high schools, colleges and universities have long played a leading role.

The education-communications problem and its solution require continuing discussion. Much more important than that, any forth-coming solutions may be the good results that could come from numerous responsible persons in both fields working together. Thus the general recommendations for action in this book are implied rather than urged in Chapters 1 through 7. They are openly and optimistically exhibited throughout Chapter 8 in a preview of the future potential of education. The challenge is vividly presented, and the goal is high.

2

EDUCATIONAL SCHIZOPHRENIA

A college sophomore with a brilliant mind recently left the dean's office for the last time. She had described her disillusionment with the campus, sworn that formal learning had no value and quit her classes. Her action received no newspaper publicity and went unnoticed by most of her classmates. Her parents were moved to little more than mild comment on family social status and a tuition refund. The professors noted her repeated absence from classes and checked her name off the roster as "dropped, passing."

Two bright high school students sat at a refreshment counter in a drugstore waiting for a prescription. Just as the physician and pharmacist aim to keep people healthy, they reasoned, the educator aims to create and sustain educated people. Yet the physician does not say to every human being aspiring to health: "You must register at my office and follow specified steps." Nor does the pharmacist suggest that a normal human will be healthier through consumption of the packaged mixtures from the drug counter rather than from natural foods, exercise and sunshine. How then, they wondered, can the professional educator encourage a system that makes education obtainable only through four years of high school followed by two or more years of preordained college courses?

A former student had turned his back on education because he was convinced that "educated person" was a fraudulent label on today's graduates. He held that popular opinion is in grave error to consider educated a person who has merely registered, paid the tuition fee, followed the plan of study and received a degree. He asserted that it is often this same person who cares not at all that good literature goes unread, good music goes unheard, and good films and television productions go unviewed, while bad media offerings are everywhere received. There are exceptions, this student admitted, but he could not recall any.

His roommate's words in a research paper were more to the point: "I have met too many holders of too many degrees who were dull on intellectual subjects, passive in social affairs, and retrogressive on most everything. They make me sick." The roommate quoted from H. L. Mencken's book, *Prejudices*: "Two-thirds of the professors in our colleges are simply cans full of undigested knowledge, mechanically acquired; they cannot utilize it; they cannot think."[1] "Liberal arts study," he continued, "is a mystical hocus-pocus charted by the dignitaries of the educational bureaucracy as a bait for student recruits and a disguise for the lecturer's specialisms." He also quoted Robert Louis Stevenson's reference to books in *An Apology for Idlers*: "Classes are good enough in their own way, but they are a mighty bloodless substitute for life."[2]

Two students were discussing a Walkabout movement mentioned in an education course. They regarded it as an effort to reconcile the extreme alternatives to schooling that a few educational critics have proposed versus such longstanding policies as the required study of certain basic courses, required attendance in specified schools for specified periods of time, and even compulsory attendance laws. Excited about the prospect of a more immediate employment rather than plodding through two or four years of college formal study, they decided to explore further such opportunities.

From another student came this regret: "Get rid of these fancy air-conditioned buildings, wide sidewalks and leafy trees—these textbooks, credit hours, labs and teaching machines. Tell the admissions and scholarship salesman I'm sorry I ever met him. Back to the hi-fi, *Playboy*, and the paperbacks."

In an open letter to the campus newspaper, still another student officially resigned from a university. He found that he could get through the courses and still not develop a sense of educational self-respect. From a television interview program, he recalled a factory worker well versed in art and a barber who knew all the answers about opera. At a public library lecture, he had met a novelist who never considered completion of college. In admiration of Abraham Lincoln and Harry S. Truman and novelists William Faulkner and Ernest Hemingway, he said, "If they can be educated with little or no actual schooling, so can I." He asserted that a barrel of sheepskins would never guarantee a literary creation or even a good life.

In Southeast Asia the frantic war in Vietnam is in the past, but neither the long years of seesaw military operations nor the final surrender of Saigon can be satisfactorily rationalized by the liberal arts and general studies. Students and other citizens found little or no means either for justifying the war or for calling the attention of the public and educators to their misgivings over the war. Some threatened to douse themselves with gasoline and strike a match. As shown in news pictures and dramatized in Erich Weller's play, *The Moon Children*, their screams, they hoped, would stir men of good will to peace on earth. Without such radiance for other causes of insufferable frustration, an alarming number of students have resorted to simpler means of suicide, through the use of drugs and over-indulgence in alcohol.

Such students are not fictitious. They are among thousands of disillusioned youth. They are the dropouts, the marchers and the rioters of the late 1960s and the early 1970s. But mostly they are bright and motivated youth in search of meaning for the mind. This chapter and those to follow comprise no attempt to explain or resolve student unrest or student apathy, nor do they suggest that the campus ferment of one generation differs sharply from that of preceding generations.[3] Least of all are these examples meant to suggest that youth as a group merit any adulation for their independence or that disrespect or scorn on their parts is justifiable. The effort here is to note a few illustrations of campus disenchantment and secession from campus life on the part of young adults who are capable of achieving a college education and to anticipate the mass media alternative for that purpose. Serious-minded students in high schools and colleges mean business. In order to prove this, they have sought satisfaction at times in what has been misrepresented as a counterculture.

In their search for honest learning, some of the students think only of rejecting their opportunities and rebelling against the Establishment. For every student who follows through with such action, there are two disenchanted parents, numerous disenchanted relatives and friends, and thousands of confused citizens. It takes patience for them to realize that these students, with rare exceptions, are neither irresponsible nor hotheaded; they are intelligent and concerned. Although willing and able to learn, they decide that college is intellectual isolation and embellished humbug. They are bored stiff, to use their own expression, and they are wondering whether equivalent learning is not more efficiently obtainable outside the traditional school system.

To a large extent the media appear to have chosen a path of aggravating the situation. They carry expose' after expose'about dope, sex and violence on the campus, all sensational copy that sells. They choose to show the hate-filled faces of alleged college students on the six o'clock news as they threaten to blow something up, or carry obscene signs, or make obscene gestures. Yet, as E. Lee McLean observed at a meeting of the American Association of State Colleges and Universities in 1970, they did not note that the more typical college student was hunched over his desk in study at all hours, and that only a very small percent of campuses witnessed disorder and violence.[4]

A Strange Separation

The view that a deliberate separation exists between formal and informal education in some cases reflects immature or naive professional understanding; in others, cloudy thinking. But many a bright person, young and old alike, feels that educators try to establish and maintain a monopoly on education. Young people complain that the prescribed steps of course-taking and degree-getting make for a false dichotomy in educational life, and, at times, a cleavage among mental functions. Students are forced to live in two incompatible worlds of learning, each irrelevant from the other.[5]

Education tends to become almost exclusively that which follows from the pursuit of state-approved lesson plans and traditional methods of classroom lecture, assignment, study, discussion, recitation and examination. It has little or nothing to do with an individual's absorption of knowledge and wisdom through outside, off-campus media such as newsstand paperbacks, magazines, newspapers, recordings, movies, radio and television.

The evidence, of course, shows that some educators are aware of the value of the mass media in the daily lives of every citizen and of the possibility of using them for self-improvement. Certainly the book medium is almost sacredly regarded, and "outside" reading is considered virtuous—and usually essential to passing a course. In addition, the fact that the basic technology of the other mass media is used within the classroom indicates an awareness of their potential. How, then, can anyone justifiably snub recognition of the educational benefits that are available outside the classroom?

In part, the separation derives from ineptly exercising the necessary force of professional standards. It stems from the artificial effort to proclaim and maintain a sharp distinction between the genuine and the nongenuine, the licensed and the nonlicensed. Thus, on campus, the line between curricular and noncurricular is fairly clear; official convocations and approved organizations may be "educational" to a degree, but they are not to be confused with the really serious endeavor of course-taking. Subject matter is officially designated "educational" when it is obtained from textbooks, lectures, syllabi or library.

The educator has lobbied loudly enough for his professional distinctions, and industry and government have taken note. In printed matter, book publishers still sharply divide educational from commercial sales.

Favored postal rates are sought for packages that are being sent from or to an educational institution. Recordings are considered educational when they are advertised as teaching aids. Radio is considered educational when it is owned and operated by an educational institution. In defining educational television, a foundation report included "all programs of an educational or cultural nature that are broadcast over educational stations."[6]

Student collections of books and recordings are lauded; on one campus they may be entered in contests. But such achievement is customarily kept outside the realm of course work. Educators praise outside reading, but are discomfited by one who veers too much from the textbook. "The newspaper in the classroom" is acceptable subject matter for an institute in teacher training, but, except for scattered group subscriptions and isolated experimentation, newspapers receive little endorsement in the general studies curriculum of high schools or colleges. A professor gives frequent assignments making use of mass market magazines, radio and television programs in order to convey a liberal understanding of American life, but a traditionalist colleague hopes that such a deviationist will be severed from the institution. A dean was dismissed after harshly criticizing the bumbling classroom performances of classroom teachers, contrasting them with fast-paced television programs.[7]

Professional educators generally endorse the world of publishing and recommend visits to bookstores with large stocks. At the same time, they establish their own college and university presses and their own book outlets on campus which are, oddly enough, sometimes filled more with sweatshirts and novelties than with books. Excellent printed aids are provided by dozens of commercial publishers, but the high school faculties never cease duplicating competitive readings, syllabi, manuals and even reprints of standard and commercially available literature. Only occasionally do educators applaud the better feature pictures and documentaries in downtown theaters and the better programs on radio and television. They prefer to favor elaborate audiovisual centers and radio-television studios that they themselves operate.

However separate, campus sponsorship of the media has a bright side. Privately owned and controlled media facilities frequently serve vital objectives. By setting up their own presses and studios, educators begin to appreciate the liberalizing and generalizing possibilities of mass media techniques. A glance at two notable journals, *Educational Broadcasting* and *Educational Broadcasting International,* as well as at publications by UNESCO and a viewing of Educational Television (ETV) and Public Broadcasting Service (PBS) programs, promptly will impress the reader with the efforts of educational promoters to break out of a shell of isolation and to amplify the voice of learning and enlarge its audience.

Still, with notable exceptions, much educational media production is either tightly geared to limited campus needs or remains crippled by other restrictive behaviors of staid pedagogy and classroom presentation methods. The stigma of "educational" media is obvious to most of the general public. Without a far greater understanding of the commercial media's superb techniques, the ventures of educators repeatedly risk such criticism as in the following comments about a university television series:

> In case you missed the two offerings shown on Channel 5, they had professors talking about science yesterday. These people have a dismal habit of talking about "areas" and "levels" and a gift for speaking sometimes as if they were patented jargon machines. They also have the curious gift of asking a question which could scarcely be phrased clearly, let alone answered, in a half-hour show, such as "Do Scientists deal in values or merely objective facts?" If they play the tape of this program, they will see the shifts of meaning given the same words. This sort of question, apart from being utterly meaningless and wasting people's time, is not very interesting. Also, it is irksome to listen to people of obviously considerable brains who have nothing better to say to a question about the atom than to point out that there are also antibiotics. Do they suppose we are unaware of it?

Even more frequent and vehement is a public dread of the very word "education," whether it be progressive or traditional, as dull, good-for-nothing stuff. This dread is sometimes accompanied by disgust with teachers and a distaste for all learning. To some individuals the educational profession and its institutions have no better reason for existence than that of being criticized for their lack of positive or practical services.

Unfortunately a large number of educators who have apparently lost a sense of direction for liberal-general education have catered to the public disillusionment and written books and articles attacking the schools. It is a professional disgrace when educators let themselves become so confused or misled as to jump on the temporary bandwagons without concern for the implications of their statements.

Both educators and media people alike have helped to bring on so desultory and obfuscating a phenomenon as McLuhanism. McLuhan himself represents a case of split personality in his attention to both public education and the public media, for his education comes from the formal structure and system of the university, and he himself is a professor of English. Still, he is so obsessed with his own conceptualization of terms such as "medium massage," "involvement," "role-playing," and "ego-gratification" that he has little or no time for other highly acceptable views on educational and social structure. Coupling his bold writings with extensive lecture and television appearances, including such commercialized assistance as a recording entitled, "Whatcha doin' Marshall McLuhan," he appears to many as a manufactured star. He freely let a pop culture develop around his name, almost according him the status of a *guru*. With due respect to his prolific thought and writing, they represent for most people a confusion between public media and public education; they merely widen a gap sorely in need of bridging. The astonishing growth of his reputation, according to a book about him by Jonathan Miller, reflects "the way in which intellectual prestige is promoted within the network of modern communications."[9]

"The message that the classroom transmits," declares a professor of education, "is that education must go on in a special room, must be directed from an external source, proceeds in a single direction (called 'forward'), and comes in fragmented sequences which can be strung together in linear fashion (usually down the hall of a school) . . . . The message is 'pay attention,' but the teacher-driver is usually riding backwards."

The classroom has windows, Robert Sidwell notes, but "the windows are not used to look outside." The classroom medium is far more than mere tedium, he concludes, "it is deadly for teachers and students alike."[10] The plea is for greater sensitivity and greater intimacy in the teacher-learner process, in order to prevent its being overshadowed by an intoxication with mass media "message" language and the determination to debunk education. The fact remains that no one comes near to spelling the death of the classroom.

Common to all hasty reproach of formal education is an unwillingness or inability to coordinate the ideas of education with the realities of an imperfect world. The thoughtless critic takes the esoteric view that education has, of necessity, been removed from the more practical, efficient, mundane, and enjoyable side of human endeavor. In a sense, such a critic suffers from a high degree of illiteracy that leads him either to identify his education erroneously with the classroom only or to fail in acknowledging what the classroom does contribute as a liaison with society. The critic has formally learned to hear, observe, and read, but he exercises none of these skills on the educational potential outside the classroom that is still nonetheless campus-related.

Those who operate and work for the mass media seem undisturbed by the peculiar isolationism of the educational world. This thinking is especially dichotomous, according to Frank Stanton of CBS, when sponsorship or objectives are in question, as when the view is taken that the educational sphere must be independent of subsidy from the commercial sphere.[11] Where publishers have organized classroom newspaper projects to help youngsters get more out of the newspaper than baseball and comics, a primary objective is also to make the students regular newspaper subscribers. When nationwide commercial television networks present programs such as "Meet the Press" or "VD Blues," they do so to fulfill in dramatic fashion a part of the public service requirement necessary for maintaining their licenses. In these and similar ventures, many media people seem to be thinking of professional education as desirable but harmless.

Those who make public communication their profession rarely solicit the educator's participation or utilize such helpful suggestions as he may make, except, of course, in technological or other circumscribed areas, or where government or foundation funding occurs. Preschool programs such as "Sesame Street" or "Electric Company" or "New Zoo Review" benefit from some educator input, but even here educators themselves hint that the results of their efforts may be anything but educational.[12]

A notable exception on television was Professor Frank Baxter who had an impressive knowledge of Shakespeare. He communicated classroom education well. But the television programmers apparently missed the significance of this success and exploited him merely as another personality. Relatively little use has been made of the fact that almost every university and college has more than one "Frank Baxter." He may be a Shakespearean authority; just as likely he may be a stimulating expert in politics, taxes, health or piano. With the slightest encouragement and guidance from a station program manager, he is ready and able to educate attractively off campus as well.

Newspapers and mass market magazines customarily give slight attention to utilizing the educator's talents. In the autumn, editors must be especially aware that children are starting school again, and that many young people are seeking guidance in choosing a college or university. On occasion, an educator may be asked to contribute to one of the newspaper supplements about education. Yet the media appear reluctant, if one compares the amount of space and time given to politics, personalities and sports. The unblushing possibility of devoting an entire issue to education hardly seems to cross an editor's mind. As in the case of television, radio, recordings and movies, editors usually select topics related to impulsive mass demand, and they predigest and enfold their presentation into a short-attention-span pabulum. Any regular reporting is about *education*, and then, only if it is newsworthy, which often means bizarre.

The least-hesitant respect for the talent and skills of the educator comes from the makers of mass market paperback books. Not only are the newsstand paperbacks carrying works from the academic realm, but the decision of what to publish for the popular market is to some extent made with educators' collaboration. Although the educational titles are far fewer in number than those with sensational overtones, it bodes well that public acceptance and retailer interest continue to support a measure of educational content.

EDUCATOR EXAMINATION

Since effective education is the business and responsibility of educators, one must turn back to them for answers to the unhappy dilemma created by mutual distrust between academics and the media. They have many answers, and they know how to find more. They should be willing to examine carefully any allegation of indifference, ingratitude and even disrespect toward what the commercial media have long been trying to do educationally. In a journal on improving teaching, Ralph Thompson admitted, "Students who cry 'Irrelevant!' often have just cause. In whole or in part many courses just do not relate; they do not constitute anything of significance for living, any part of a viaticum for life."[13]

Educator criticism has increasingly pointed to the vast difference between the modern home environment of electronic communications intake and the classroom. As McLuhan points out about television, children are so attuned to up-to-the-minute, adult news—inflation, rioting, war, taxes, crime and bathing beauties—that they are bewildered by the school environment "where information is scarce but ordered and structured by fragmented, classified patterns, subjects and schedules."[14] In a similar vein, Robert Hilliard, an educational critic, has complained: "All children today, including and maybe especially the ghetto child, live in an aural and visual world. Yet, virtually every education program in the country is rooted in the print world of fifty years ago."[15] Such observations are seldom followed by meaningful resolutions, however, or by the necessary professional confidence in self and others.

From a sociological analysis of the interplay of social structure, high culture and mass culture, Harold Wilensky concludes that those who have confidence in the major institutions of American society distrust television and radio networks and those who trust the media distrust other institutions.[16] If it is impossible for the educator to find a way to accept media help in commercial ventures and still trust the sponsor, then it is impossible to trust the pluralist or multigroup society in which we live. Poor quality in mass media fare is not necessarily an accompaniment to commercial interests. If countless thousands are settling for pig swill, it is largely because educators have not set a place for them at the king's table. Indeed, the educator should ask whether his obligation is not one of coordinating the leadership for enlightenment.

Undue concern about separation ignores the fact that the production and the distribution of educational content both in and out of the schoolroom are very much part of a mixed system. Even the educational service of the mass media operates under a mixed system of commercial and noncommercial sponsorship. The production of textbooks and other teaching devices is a task of the business world as much as is the manufacture of building materials or sweeping compound. Television and radio emanating from the campus need "the facilities and unlimited monies for trial and error of the nets and local commercial stations"[17]—money that educators do not normally command.

And when an educator actually works with the glamorous mass media, he may try to draw up the message, purpose and content quite on his own. With blind faith in his professional wares, he may forget all the demands of the public for appealing content—a claim must be considered in at least the initial stages of education. He may look upon popular nonacceptance as bigotry, rather than realizing that people may be merely unconvinced or bored.

The overzealous educator may envision a regional, national or even world system of educational services and influence under the teaching profession. He might imagine an educational superstructure powerful enough to counteract the destructive effects of purely commercial media, to still the voice and force of lay opposition. Such thoughts, when spoken, provoke a student into a suspicious attitude with regard to his professors and the media.

Student demonstrations, sit-ins and lay-ins express intense demands for change on the campus front. They hit at tuition hikes, examinations, faculty cuts, service curtailments, as well as other ways in which the budget is handled. The destruction of property, imprisonment of officials, and oration of obscenities are but a crude way of shouting disaffection with vapid teaching. In the 1960s, historian Arnold Toynbee observed that the Establishment's poor performance was mainly due not to ill will but to self-complacency, to distraction by the extreme pressure of life, and to the recent huge increase in numbers and magnitudes which tends to make social relations impersonal.[18]

As enrollment steadily declined in the 1970s, campus performance appeared no more impressive. Administrators sought every means to attract and hold enough students to justify the existence of, and merit financial support for, their institution. Faculty members compromised grading standards by generously apportioning A's and B's with little regard for evidence of learning.[19] Potential employers especially found that the college years of an applicant accorded him little or no difference in terms of employability over one who had not attended college. When a record of high grades revealed a student of poor caliber, campuses were accused of grade inflation. As in the 1960s, educators frustrated not only employers, but parents and other citizens as well.

The mass media add to the confusion and slip from common sense when they attempt to ride the educational rail without the educator. Unconcerned and unaccountable for evaluating student performance, they nonetheless disseminate information. It is especially distressful in the di-

gressing analysis of a news event, which might best be left to straight reporting. J.B. Priestly wrote that the media make so much of "nothing" or,
at best, of the obvious, that often when "something" occurs, it is almost
too much to bear. In such a situation, he continues: "The commentators
are half out of their minds. It's here—something! So they begin flogging
it to death or hammering it into the ground. A tape is looked at from
above, below, from all sides. It is taken to pieces and then put together
again. It is passed through finer and finer sieves. It is examined and commented upon by every kind of expert, with everything represented except
perhaps ordinary common sense."[20] It is inevitable, as Priestly concluded, that many of us are groaning with boredom, and that we suffer
from relentless overcommunication. The medium truly becomes tedium.

Overcommunication quickly became a major problem in the Watergate coverage. Newsworthy and significant for a brief time, the successful
effort of media communicators to string it out and keep it alive, bolstered
by varied political forces and retributions, contributed directly to the declining of the image of the United States abroad and, in turn, to a host of
economic defeats for the citizenry. In the aftermath, economic woes could
hardly compete with Watergate for scandal and sensationalism. The situation for the newsmongers is much like a post-wartime peace that sneaks
up, leaving the media uncertain over how their public wants them to
handle it.

"Besides the deprivation to television viewers and armchair strate-
gists," an editorial in *Barron's* stated, "it [peace] stacks up as a cruel
trauma to those kindly hearts whose every waking hour has been self-
lessly dedicated to demonstrating against one way or another. . . . What
an abrupt and abysmal void in their lives. And, closer to home (in a professional sense), what's ahead for those gallant heirs of Hemingway, who
have been covering wars in open-throated mufti for the newspapers or
Time or TV? A fire in Hoboken, the ups and downs of pork bellies in Chicago, a school board meeting in Santa Barbara? Small potatoes, we're
afraid, after filing on the last days of Phnom Penh or how the Turks
took Cyprus."[21]

Do the media need an editorial writer, or anyone else, to plead, "Will
somebody please start another war or, at least, another Watergate?" There
must be a place for the tempering perspective of the learned educator in
this frantic, separatist pursuit of public attention through an inadvertent
educative role.

An uncompromising separatist attitude held by educators and the
media and the pragmatic necessity for a mixed system form a paradox.
The educator has a rich fund of commercial resources available, but much
of it he chooses to ignore as not quite passing the test of pedagogy or other
traditional classroom standards. On the other hand, he guards the riches

of his offerings closely, doling them out in curricularly prescribed portions. At the same time, the brighter classroom student knows that widely available commercial print, disc, tape, film, sound frequencies, and co-axial cable abound in educational content. He justifiably may complain of a case of schizophrenia in the educational system. To paraphrase Lyman Bryson's observation years ago of society's being dragged in opposite directions, and conflicts in ideals and standards of value between the media and teaching threatens to perpetuate a schizophrenic society.

In brief, a rift has occurred between the formal pursuit of education and the informal educational effect of the mass media. A decline in the general vigor and clarity of purposeful educational endeavor has ironically accompanied the far-reaching technological developments of mass communications. Behind a communications revolution that appears too swift, the revolutionary potential of academic institutions is too slow. Education itself has fallen between these two revolutions of contrasting pace and often conflicting paths, and with it, the bulk of teachers, students, and other citizens.

3

A REVOLUTION
TOO SWIFT—
COMMUNICATIONS

Revolution is a frequently used word. In the United States people celebrate the results of the American Revolution on July 4 each year. The Bicentennial Celebration in 1976 was planned and widely publicized long in advance. Many Americans have also heard of Bastille Day on July 14, a day that commemorates the French Revolution. People frequently read in newspapers of coups and new regimes in other countries. Moreover, whenever a public speaker raises a distress signal about rapid innovation and sudden upheaval in social, economic, scientific, or intellectual arenas, he is implying revolution. The speaker is generally referring to a radical, widespread change in administration or attitude. In each case, it is undergirded by the revolution in communications.

Whereas, centuries ago the weapons of physical force were widely presumed to be the only certain way to capture power in state and society, today a successful coup d'etat benefits from the combined weapons of press, radio, television, film and recording. Their darts pierce the public so deeply that they are prone to constant manipulation of people's thinking. In combination, the media have forged the most powerful instrument ever devised for changing or molding the minds and behavior of people. A fast-paced revolution in itself, public communications has also had a profound revolutionary effect on other segments of society; its influence will continue to grow. Its sound definition for the educator and educational supporter and critic is vital.

21

THE NATURE OF PUBLIC COMMUNICATIONS

Communication that is direct requires only two persons—one who speaks, writes or gestures and one who listens, reads or observes. Called person-to-person or interpersonal communications, it presumes a degree of direct proximity, if not acquaintance, between the two parties involved. It is not "public" in the mass media sense. Interpersonal communication also occurs in an auditorium, theater, or stadium—any place where audience and communicator are both gathered in the flesh. Despite the largeness of the audience in such a setting, the term "in person" or "personal appearance" is clearly meaningful. A single audience physically assembled together is limited in size by the area of the gathering place. Lacking amplification systems, Athenians in Aristotle's time called a group gathered within the range of an orator's voice the "natural community."

Until recently, a large measure of volition was presumed whenever communication at an assembly took place. If an individual chose not to send or receive a communication, he could isolate himself. He or she could leave a group that had an unappealing spokesman and could easily escape from a captive audience by merely wandering away. It was relatively easy to choose the life of a hermit, far removed from compelling messages to consume and succeed.

In contrast, modern mechanical and electronic media allow little or no evasion of the communicative acts that are very literally and thoroughly "public." Countless, anonymous people are confronted every hour of the day through television, radio, motion pictures, recordings and the press. Today an individual cannot escape public spokesmen who never cease demanding that he be happy and successful. No longer able to congregate in a single place within the unmagnified range of a human voice, huge audiences in the shrinking world of the twentieth century represent a new "natural community," a "global village." The philosopher Ortega y Gasset referred to a rising tide of masses capable of revolt.[1] As such audiences in the mass, they certainly carry revolutionary impact.

Since mid-twentieth century, for the first time in recorded history, a communicator's words or gestures can instantly and simultaneously reach millions of listeners and viewers. Mass communications, coined "masscom" by textbook author Don Pember, is the most colorful, exciting and controversial of the several worlds in which we live today—"a world of magic carpets and fairylands."[2] It forges a nation and its people. It has the shape of a megaphone: any of its messages, emanating from a single source, is beamed to an infinitely large number of people with such speed that a pause for intelligent, liberal reflection becomes difficult and infrequent.

TODAY'S MOST DYNAMIC INSTITUTION

Human relatedness literally around the globe is the keystone of the modern media of public communications. Steam-driven and rotary presses, linotype, photoengraving, electromatic typesetting, telegraph, telephone, and wireless—these were revolutionary inventions for communication in the period between mid-nineteenth and early twentieth centuries. They were necessary innovations that made possible today's daily exchange of human experience by means of television, film, radio, records and tapes, newspapers, magazines, and books. Millions now hear, see, speak and read over long distances more rapidly and frequently than was ever dreamed of a half-century or even a few decades ago. Person-to-person or face-to-face contact is no longer essential for togetherness. Humans are bound together, although in an impersonal and often depersonalized sense, by modern mass communications.

The range of the human senses of hearing and sight has been extended immeasurably. Until recently, trumpets, bells, drums and guns were among the limited range of signals that people used to communicate, whereas modern codes of the submarine cable and telegraph now traverse oceans and continents. The human voice, once limited to the range of human hearing, now reaches to the farthest points of the earth via telephone and radio. Sight signals by smoke, beacons, flags, semaphores and rockets have been superseded by satellite television and radio. Words and pictures simultaneously reach human ears and eyes throughout the world. Potentially, they create an open faucet, pouring out knowledge.

Who can guess what future research will yield? The exchange of signals and voices between earth and moon and satellites already has been achieved; intergalactic messages are imminent. What additional—and presently unknown—communications techniques are yet to appear? Already, printed advertisements can give off special aromas. How long will it be before people enjoy "smellevision" or "feelevision"? What role will a more highly developed extrasensory perception play in future communications efforts? Will we experience in our homes something like an Advent Screen, as predicted by John Bradshaw in "The Shape of Media Things to Come—A Science-Fiction Story That's All True," a device that will permit information to be transmitted by light when one is asleep, so that on waking one will already have "read" the news?[3]

Transportation is a vital aid to modern communications. Runners, riders and pigeons have yielded to trains, planes and faster ships that now join every conceivable outpost of human civilization. Modern transportation makes possible the physical pickup and delivery necessary to build and maintain the movie, radio and television installations and feed them the films, recordings and scripts for thousands of daily programs. The transportation system daily distributes billions of books, periodicals and newspapers. Modern carriers efficiently transport the people who animate the web of communications.

Technology in communications and transportation have the potential to alter human lives radically. More efficient sources of power from atomic energy, the sun, the tides and winds are predicted. As people have bent nature to their will, they have manipulated the process of life and loosened the chains of gravity binding them to the earth. Electronics has freed the mind for life in what has been called the "Intellectronic Age." It enables a computer to transmit all the contents of an encyclopedia in three minutes, while technicians can repair the "brain" of Telstar at a distance of 2,500 miles. The fairyland of developments has combined to increase production and income, while simultaneously increasing the potential for more and safer births and longer life spans, greater personal wealth and a higher standard of living for everyone.

The home of tomorrow may focus on a "communicenter," comparable to central heating, with branches leading to every room, and even reaching out to the individual when he leaves the house. As early as 1958, Maurice B. Mitchell, President of Encyclopedia Britannica Films, envisioned communications-oriented families with each member wearing a two-way portable radio on his wrist.[4] Every telephone will show a picture of the person with whom one is conversing and every television will be two-way. All of this, including color photo copy and recorded sound copy, might be part of a home console and computer terminal. In a "Happy Bicentennial" article, Joan Kron describes replacement of the traditional fireplace-oriented family room with the media room. "Today's revolution is communications in the home," she asserts. "What with the televisions, telephones, hi-fidelity sets, citizen-band radios, slides, movies, not to mention computer terminals and the Telex, the home is getting to look like the control room of NewsCenter 4."[5]

In a book attempting to answer the question of who is shaping the picture of the world, Robert Stein foresees the prospect of future newspapers that will consist mainly of headlines and brief summaries and future magazines that will consist largely of brochures on a variety of new developments.[6] They will enhance an electronic trinity of cables, cassettes and computers. The specific form of media projection—giant television screen or paper printout—will become less important than the change of relationship between information gatherer (editor, publisher, broadcaster) and information recipient (reader, listener, viewer). The latter will switch from a passive position to an active one of shopping and enjoying only what is wanted. Making use of the memory storage of the computer, the process will allow an individual to order an editorial, old movie, kiddie show, baseball game, or symphony concert to suit genuinely personal interest.

In a still more omnipresent and revolutionary network of communications, unhappily, are interwoven horrendous inferences for its unscrupulous exploitation. All-powerful political bosses and their army of managers could subject a population to slavery. In the brave new world described by Aldous Huxley, ministries of propaganda, newspaper editors and school teachers make people love their servitude. In the Newspeak language of George Orwell's book, *1984*, are elegantly lettered slogans bombarding everyone with the love of Big Brother, with the spirit of "victory over himself." With no more independence than trained dogs jumping through hoops, consumers are already conditioned to respond unconsciously to the manipulations of psychology and motivational research in highly advertised soaps, creams, deodorants, cigarettes, beers and automobiles.[7]

Throughout the continuing communications revolution, each citizen must avoid being the mere awe-stricken observer, technician or science promoter exclaiming "Long live Paradise!" For there is nothing in the technology to insure against transmutation of blessings into curses, servant into master, hope into terror. Despite promises, nothing in the trends guarantees ease or truth or goodness in human relations, whether personal, familial, social, national or international. As has been said of other instrumentalities of human persuasion and power, the mass media can serve the Devil as well as the Lord. Precisely in such mechanical neutrality, however, lies the challenge to communicator and educator.

In the new world of time, speed and convenience, labor and management discuss a four-day work week. A thirty-two-hour schedule would mean more leisure time. It is understandable for a civic leader to ask whether leisure-bent people will continue to reach for trivialities and escape through television and radio, through a spectator role at the movies, and through the soporific adoption of newspapers, to be used along with millions of automobiles and a billion gallons of liquor.[8] Will it be rare for the idle minds to be filled with thoughts of value? Will its doors be opened for wider enlightenment or permanently closed by a devastating monster of narrowly influential and controlling interests?

Almost every group, organization and institution—public and private—already proclaims its message as representative or significant for everyone. For many the effect is one of confusion, an almost hopeless jumble of viewpoints, a babble of barking voices, a scramble of jigsaw pieces, sometimes on the path to a nightmare. One student described his world as "pictures, words and music everywhere but not a stop to think." For only a few persons of superior intellectual and moral application do the unique qualities of individual media combine in a coherent pattern. They should be coherent and enriching for millions more; this book helps to show how this can be.

Whether enlightenment, enjoyment, horror or indifference ultimately stems from the public mass media depends also on the capacity of the individual member of the audience to make intelligent use of the offerings. His skill in reading is basic here, as are his taste and judgment during exposure to content via all media. His general familiarity with many fields of knowledge is indispensable to forming an organized pattern that is rich and rewarding. Concern for the individual human being enveloped by mass communication, for his hopes and fears, for its numerous devices and for the cultural context continue to be subjects of penetrating research. Universities foster departments and schools that concentrate on media problems; national foundations and professional organizations lend research attention; the communications industries survey their effectiveness and improvement, and government frantically seeks proper regulation and legislation.

COMMUNICATIONS AND GOVERNMENT

In the complex and populous societies of today, mass communications provide most of the cohesion for the functioning of an integrated and interdependent society. A network of understandings and contacts enable government of the modern community to exist. In turn, the purposes of the media, their content and the controls imposed upon them reflect the fundamental principles of the societies and governments for whom they function.

The theories underlying the use of the media echo shifts in social and political environment between authoritarianism and democracy. Governments have used their powers to limit or suppress discussion, to encourage better and more extensive communication and to be parties to the process of communication.[9] Although radio and television, film and recordings are products of a twentieth-century climate of democracy, the older media of pamphlets, books, newspapers and periodicals were developed under authoritarian influences.

To the English monarchs of the sixteenth and seventeenth centuries, the printed media functioned to support and advance government. Permission to own a printing press was a privilege for which the owner acknowledged an obligation of loyalty to the policies of the crown. This early authoritarian concept of the function of the mass media has had the widest and longest acceptance throughout the world. It survives today in states where the press operates to bolster the existing power wielders of the state and owes to them its privileges of existence. To a large extent, authoritarianism characterizes many information agencies in government.

According to the communist theory of the twentieth century, all mass communications are instruments for governmental and political action. The state owns and operates the mass media as a positive force to accomplish its policies through directing thought and expression. Communicators, teachers, librarians, intellectuals and other leaders in the community and the nation are enlisted in the mass media for one purpose: to aid the revolutionary dictatorship of the proletariat in extending socialism and eventually building communism. A communist regime exploits every potential of communications to propagate the revolutionary cause. The Soviet press, for example, is first and foremost beholden to the Communist Party and the government bureaucratic apparatus.[10]

The idea of a press independent of government authority began to develop only after the political revolution of 1688 in England when Parliament successfully proclaimed freedom from a tyrannical kingship. John Milton made an eloquent plea against government licensing of printed matter. John Locke insisted upon individual liberty and reasoned that government authority must be a mere trusteeship. The rapidly changing philosophy held that people were rational beings possessing inherent natural rights including the right to pursue truth, which civil or religious authority could not jeopardize. Systematized and popularized further by Enlightenment thinkers in the eighteenth century, these rights found expression in the Declaration of Independence and in the United States' Constitutional provision for freedom of speech, press and religion.

Gradually the democratic base of political power widened as did the acceptance of religious toleration and economic freedom. John Stuart Mill, in the nineteenth century, emphasized that the smallest minority should have as much freedom of expression as the most powerful majority, and that the dignity of the individual is inviolate. Rather than automatically supporting the government, the free press was to inform the public about activities affecting the general welfare and expose any questionable government policies. Press communications were to be instruments of accurate and authoritative information and comment.

With the communications revolution of the early twentieth century, the press was transformed into the big business of the powerful mass media. Milton, Jefferson, Mill, Holmes and others had asserted that truth is found and tested in a free and competitive marketplace of information and ideas, and that a free "self-righting process" was preferable to censorship and regulation. Now the impact of nationwide newspaper and magazine syndicates, networks, movie house chains and other possible monopolistic combinations complicates what had emerged as a relatively simple freedom. The determination of truth from among numerous conflicting evidences and alternatives became far more difficult—and raised the prospect of once again controlling the media, but this time, in order to facilitate democracy rather than to defend authority.

In mid-twentieth century a Commission of Freedom of the Press warned that the legal right of managers of the mass media to expand would remain unaltered only if their moral duty and social responsibility were performed. The libertarian position, stressing protection of the media from governmental tyranny, had developed into a concern that the government protect readers, listeners and viewers from the media's power. The media industry's freedom from the control of government became the people's freedom to know under the protection of government. A new theory of social responsibility responded to the need to help a citizen distinguish between truth and falsehood and to be better informed and better represented, especially if he was from a minority part of the constituency.

The difficult question of where the protection of government and politics coincide came to the surface dramatically in a nationwide address in 1969 by former Vice President Spiro Agnew. He attacked what he called "the tiny and closed fraternity of privileged men" who prepared, packaged and interpreted the news that forty million Americans receive each night. He charged that the media favored political liberals, placed undue emphasis on gore and violence, built obscure agitators into celebrities and poisoned the public against the government. While *Time* and *Newsweek* made the claim a front-page cover story and network presidents angrily countercharged that the Vice President was trying to intimidate the newsmen, countless American citizens expressed support for Agnew's statements. More than ever before, it became evident to the public that there were media characteristics, such as deadlines and space requirements, that can influence content.[11] What can newsmen do in twelve minutes or in one column? Aware that somebody must look at how accurately the media shape the picture of society and thus educate the people, newsmen and most citizens agreed it was not the job of politicians.[12]

The media had come under suspicious scrutiny for failing to provide a free and open exchange of ideas. There was a question of monopoly. Newspapers, mass-circulation magazines, broadcast ownership and movie theaters tended to be concentrated into a few hands, and thus to manipulate public opinion by selecting the content. In an account of how the news media manipulate public opinion through bias, distortion and censorship, Robert Cirino stated: "A communication policy that gives money the power to determine who will control the mass media is *bound* to favor the political viewpoints and policies of conservative elements in society."[13] Moderates, too, he held, join in attacking sex education not based on the *Bible*, standing behind big business and the military-industrial-space-media complex and helping to give the radical right about a hundred-to-one advantage over the radical left.

The potential threat of political control of television has been thoughtfully analyzed by Newton Minow, former chairman of the Federal Communications Commission, along with associates John B. Martin and Lee M. Mitchell. In their book entitled *Presidential Television*, they describe the preeminent ability of a chief executive, commander-in-chief, White House candidate and party leader to appear simultaneously on all national radio and television networks at prime, large-audience evening hours, with no expense to government, party or self. Presidential television ranges from a news conference to light conversational banter on a popular entertainment program, always the single explanation of plans, policies, and justification regarding war, peace, praise for political allies, disfavor toward opponents and veto of legislation.[14]

This kind of assertion weakened before references to the successful removal of a president, the curtailment of funds for the Vietnam War, and the sensitivity to minority viewpoints and behavior. Former Federal Communications Commissioner Nicholas Johnson, an outspoken critic of big business influence on the media, concurred: "America does have available governmental machinery which is capable of scotching undue accumulations of power over the mass media, at least in theory and to some extent."[15]

Entertainment content of the mass media provides enjoyment and may nourish powers of aesthetic appreciation. It also helps to inform and teach. Often ignored or feared in the operation of political institutions, it has not had the preferential status that protected the information function. Antidemocratic or un-American implications of entertainment in books, films or broadcasts have at times placed their creators under scrutiny for their nonconformist views and deprived them of the full guarantees of freedom of speech and press. Courts have since held that the content of entertainment, literature and art, rather than their author or communicator, is the proper basis for judging them.

Some intelligent observers complain about blatant falsification of the fact of teamwork or the building of superstars. In disgust, they cry out when interest becomes centered on a "star" personality and ignores the value of a good performance or an original production involving many persons. The comedian, the interviewer, the disc jockey, the disc artist, the columnist and the lead player are sometimes primed up to steal the show. They are literally placed on exhibition like decorated horses at the circus.

For the sake of truth and accuracy, it has been asked, should the government play a role of requiring temperance of expenditure and effort in creating and perpetuating stars, leaving more accurately credited the role of teamwork? Should a communications medium be free to condition people year after year to cheer and laugh, to read and admire before a pre-determined focus, without ever being encouraged to consider exactly what it is that they are applauding? Similarly, where the part played by a manufactured star, as an orchestra conductor, a singer or a dancer, is grossly exaggerated, the audience is inclined to take for granted the orchestra, the composer, the chorus or troupe, the production manager, the technical staff, the announcer and a host of others. The same excess of attention on one individual and the neglect of the team apply to the stardom of actors and actresses, news commentators and authors as well.

In a sense, the obverse of the inflation of personality is the violation of personality and of individual dignity, the desecration of a human being who is much more, or should be much more, than a profit-making instrument of mass communication. The biographies of such great screen stars as Judy Garland and Marilyn Monroe reveal the employer exploitation to the point of a loss of self and of the tragedy caused by abuse from drugs. The pulp magazines and the Hollywood columnists report the star's every remark and move and fabricate it for as much effect as possible. René Maheu, Director General of UNESCO, deplores public communication breaches of good taste and social decorum, as well as outrages against the human person, which respect "neither the privacy of love or prayer nor the seclusion of poverty, neither the peace and quiet of a happy home nor the grief and sorrow of death." The purveyor of information, he holds, has government-protected freedom "only insofar as the public which he serves has the right to be informed; and the public has no right to know other people's private lives."[16]

A frequent criticism is that people are not receiving from the media as much of the important, readily usable information about society and government that is required, if they are to play a meaningful role in increasingly complex government discussions. Besides the tendency of media ownership to be concentrated in fewer and fewer hands, one may attribute this information problem to back-scratching between reporters and government officials, and to the lack of professional standards or rewards for performance. In all cases, the need to watch and even to blow the whistle on media misperformance is acute. The choices as to who should do the watching and the whistle-blowing may come from the government, the media themselves or the public. The effectiveness will depend upon a combination of the three, oriented toward the highest educational ideals.

The assurance of free and responsible mass media is a revolutionary issue calling for urgent and repeated debate and defense. Democracy ultimately rests on the assumption that people have—or may acquire—sufficient intelligence and integrity to manage their affairs with a minimum of compulsion, by free discussion and through reasonable compromise. If this assumption is valid, as the historian Carl L. Becker forcefully states in one of his lectures published in *Freedom and Responsibility*[17], then freedom of learning and teaching is essential, for it is obvious that the better informed the people are, the more likely their goals will be wise and the measures taken to attain them effective. On the validity of this assumption rests the permanent significance of the educator, and *his* ongoing revolution.

If the assumption is not valid, Becker countered, at least in the long run, then democracy is only a temporary phase of a passing revolution—a luxury available only to those fortunate enough to live in new and undeveloped countries, or in countries momentarily endowed with wealth. Then the broad-minded citizen is a fictitious character, created by educators and politicians and overwhelmed by public communicators. He is a mere *homo eruditus*, parallel to the *homo juridicus* presumed in the phrase, "No one is supposed to be ignorant of the law," but denied in the fact that almost everyone is lost in its maze. He is in formal possession of an education, but in reality he is only confused by it. He contributes little or nothing to the health of democracy in America and to its significant and ongoing revolution.

SERVICE TO THE PUBLIC

The mass media carry revolutionary potential and raise huge problems of social responsibility in their role of public service. They inform, advertise, propagandize, entertain, inspire, orient and educate. Under an authoritarian government, these functions serve to strengthen the state, its political philosophy and its socioeconomic principles. Under a democratic government respecting human freedom, the mass media are charged with these services in order to broaden the bases for political, social and economic decisions, to improve the standard of living and to enrich personal philosophies of life.

Individual enrichment and the duty of inspiring and educating lie more commonly in the province of teachers, clergymen, poets, dramatists, social workers, and statesmen. Unfortunately, they are often in conflict with the mass media in a democratic and progressive society over the issue of popular demand versus higher standards of taste and morality. "Serving the people" means, on the one hand, seeking out and responding to their demands and wishes. The phrase is often interpreted as making popular response the criterion, even when it may be mediocre or vulgar. "Serving the people" means, to many others, raising their level of taste and giving them what they need for their own basic improvement.

This conflict between popular demand and aesthetic or educational values is part of an ancient philosophical issue. It is also fundamental to the theory and practice of liberalizing and broadening the minds of the individual citizens who make up the populace. "Through liberal education," said C. Scott Fletcher, President of Educational Television and Director of the Fund for Adult Education, "the free and open society must seek not only to encourage all its individuals to want to make decisions but also to fit them to make wise and humane ones." This public responsibility, which he has emphasized with eloquence, relates the mass media directly to education.[18]

Drawing on his experience in developing countries, Wilbur Schramm described the spectacular effect of radio and print when it first entered a traditional village.[19] Almost overnight, horizons were pushed back. He wrote: "New concepts and images flow through the communication channels—crop rotation, insecticides, vaccination, elections, family planning. Power passes from the wise men who command knowledge of far away places and new methods of doing things." "Without the mass media to support and extend education and to help adults learn how to improve their level of living," Schramm added, "the development plans and schedules would not have enabled sixty new countries to come into existence."

A sober warning against this kind of wholesale revolution throughout entire countries comes from another professor, Herbert Schiller.[20] "Weak societies," he states, "are beginning to be menaced with extinction . . . from a few power centers in the industrialized world." There is a threat of media power that disseminates and establishes a chronic "cultural mush." Advertising agents and media executives, of course, chafe at the allegation that they mongrelize culture, and they hasten to point out the variety of their wares. Educators, too, benefiting from consulting assignments abroad, are less sensitive to preserving a culture than to aiding a revolutionary public communications process (and sometimes a revolutionary government) in expediting technological change that rubberstamps that purveyed by major powers.

The dilemma is heightened by the presumption of a literate populace capable of digesting and assessing information and editorial comment on public matters. It further presumes an interested and socially conscious public, aware of its part in the ongoing democratic process. But the media are enjoined not to take anything for granted: a newspaper, newsweekly, or news broadcast in the United States, therefore, is expected to present an accurate coverage of current political controversies and to offer interpretive reporting and background information so that the reader or listener may as fully as possible see implications.

Just as the public mass media have a responsibility to the public, so does the advertising world, which is supported by business and industry. In the highly integrated business and industrial system of the United States, advertising is vital: it informs the consumer about old and new products and services, and invigorates the economy by moving goods from manufacturer to retailer to consumer. In addition, "public service" or "paid" messages sell ideas, convince audiences of the soundness or unsoundness of a belief, promote safety and health, urge enactment or repeal of legislation, or rally support to a cause or a candidate. By paying for a substantial part of the cost of media operation in the United States, advertising makes television, radio, newspapers and magazines available to a far larger public at low cost.

But this does not free advertising from the restraints that apply to other media. Just as the mass media are expected to be judicious, so sales messages must be truthful, accurate, tasteful, moderate. A concern with ever larger public audiences means more than giving them everything they want or can be incited to want. The very simplicity of the "demand concept" should give us pause. "Giving the public what it wants," declared H. Carleton Greene, Director-General of the BBC, "and its too frequent use by those whose training and skill lie in cajolery of the simpleminded should make us suspicious."[21] No communicator is justified in using the voice of the people as an excuse for peddling cheap, shallow, and borderline trash, for perpetuating habits which are harmful, or for glorifying violence or criminals.

The Chinese have a saying, "If a thousand people believe a foolish thing, it is still a foolish thing." Not one iota of low-grade content is made worthwhile by the rationalization that much high-grade content is also disseminated—as if taste and values were an equation in which so much bad and so much good balanced out to an acceptable average. Nor is it acceptable to justify low-taste content because it is a key element in integrating the whole complex of the American economic and social institutions, or because catering to low taste as the largest segment of the purchasing market brings stability to the economy.[22] If true, such assertions approach the extreme laissez-faire view, which frowns upon any external regulation of the media, especially if it is governmental.

Whether the issue involves entertainment or information or the purposes and availability of the mass media, the practice in the United States has been to encourage a maximum amount of *self-regulation*. Those who own and operate the media and those who communicate the messages are expected to exercise restraint and judgment, to organize a set of standards which its members will enforce among themselves. Unlike government censorship, regulation by codes of ethics has the advantage of being self-imposed; its disadvantages become evident when the codes are ignored.

In the freedoms and responsibilities entailed in regulation and restraint, the role of the educator is basic for keeping the principles alive. Public opinion and buying behavior, the educator believes, may be influenced by media persuaders, but they must not be manipulated. The technical training of those who would communicate beneficially must be accompanied by democratic understanding, broad learning, and humanitarian inclination. Since its beginning, the United Nations Educational, Scientific, and Cultural Organization (UNESCO) has proclaimed these requirements. In 1967, its Director-General, René Maheu, stated that the time was overdue for those who controlled and worked with the media to recognize responsibilities in direct relation to the fantastic power they had either to inform or deform or to educate or stultify.[23]

Under no circumstances can an educator compromise with low standards of taste or desire. He knows that an undiscerning public largely takes what it gets and that it wants more of what is repeatedly dangled before it. In preparing for a scheduled event, a band director or a basketball coach does not ask a player whether he feels the need for intensive practice; the question is not raised. Similarly, a responsible classroom lecture is one which gives the students what they need to meet humanitarian objectives, not whatever their whims tell them that they want. The latter recourse may guide a teacher in winning fleeting popularity, but the former will yield lasting benefit for everyone.

Herein lies a principle equally binding on the responsible communicator. Along with considering all popular requests, he is also obligated to join the educator in helping to guide the public in skillful perception, wise choice and intelligent resistance to vulgarization. On the other hand, many newspaper and magazine columns and radio and television programs of counsel and instruction, ranging from maintaining health and physical fitness to exercising intelligent voting behavior and all forms of consumerism, do reflect educational responsibility. It is almost ironic, then, when anxious educators water down their classroom curricula to a level sometimes lower than the average person's intelligence. Facing the dilemma of decreasing enrollment and the loss of their job security, they resort to actions which are tantamount to betraying themselves to their cause. Instead of keeping their own objectives and standards clear while working with learning from the media, they descend to competition and compromise. By no stretch of economic logic can professors compete successfully with mass media by debasing liberal-general education, with its priceless values.

For Audiences of Millions

A medium of communication can be designated "mass" when it attracts huge numbers of participants from all parts of the country—of every age, income and educational level. A mass medium does not discriminate geographically between big cities and rural areas. It is public in the sense that it is not closed to any individual or group by reason of sex, race, religion, personal belief, or socioeconomic class. Its audiences range in variety and size from the several thousands of intellectuals who read in a popular magazine a special-interest article on ceramics in the ancient world to the millions who tune in to a broadcast of a presidential inauguration or a Rose Bowl game. The audience members are largely anonymous and depersonalized one from another.

The more hours of the day and the more forms in which a message is communicated, the more people the media can reach. For the most part the segments of content come in small packages, any one of them not intended for lasting worth. Individuals looking through a picture magazine, reading an evening newspaper or a popular book, sitting in a movie theater, or turning the dial on a radio or television set—all are the recipients in the public communications audience. The response by mail, telephone, or telegraph, their purchases of the products advertised, and the polling and sampling surveys, show that they are millions strong and in wide variety.

To reach still greater audiences of millions, a television or radio program can be taped or filmed for repeated later presentations. Although the contents of a book can be indefinitely preserved for future availabliity, the audience for a book at any one moment may be limited by the number of copies published, but the number of individuals exposed to its content is extended immeasurably when it is read or passed on to others, reprinted in periodicals, filmed or recorded. When used interchangeably and cooperatively, the mass media reach unlimited audiences.

Media outreach relies on a speed of transmission ranging from the immediacy of radio and television, to a few hours for newspaper publication and distribution, and a few days for magazines, recordings and paperback books. "Instant paperbacks" are usually written by journalists used to the rigors of newspaper or wire-service deadlines. They are often capitalizing on a momentous news event or anticipating a government crisis. The alliance of the instant paperback with the current scene and with its speedy production is a significant reason for considering the mass market paperback. Dating from a publishing revolution in 1939, when the firm of Pocket Books was founded, mass market paperbacks differ from hard-cover books by their low prices, their large first printings

(100,000 copies or more) and their distribution through magazine and newsstand outlets.[24] Reprintings soon mount. *The Valley of the Dolls*, with a total of 15,800,000 copies sold by mid-1973, replaced *Peyton Place* for the highest sales honor in the *Guinness Book of World Records*.

Technical controls of pace and speed also provide flexibility and adaptation for the many audiences. Devices permit the speeding up and slowing down of reality to a point commensurate with the limitations of the senses: recordings can play the sounds at slower or faster rates; movies can decrease or increase the speed of action. Within a five-minute film, the life cycle of a plant or an animal, the biography of a statesman, or the history of a century can be revealed. During a similar time span, the trajectory of a missile may be "drawn out," an auto accident or an athletic field play may be seen in slow motion. Photographs interspersed with written description in books and periodicals also make possible a pacing of content in forms more tangibly convenient and preservable. Media variety is irresistible.

It is characteristic of the mass media that society has abandoned none of them. Audiences use and need them all. With the coming of radio, there were fears that people would no longer read their news in newspapers; with the coming of television, alarmists were even more certain that the reading of books would become a lost art, and that publishers would go out of business. Many observers feared (some hoped) that motion pictures would vanish, and others predicted the demise of radio. For periods of time, recordings have suffered an ominous lull in sales.

It is true that there is an intermedia competition of a sort, and that preferences for one medium over another reflect social change. It is also true that some of the functions of one medium, say, the book, may be shared and even taken over by another medium. But such shifts have not displaced a process of common nourishment. Television presents Hollywood films. Magazines increase in number and circulation. Books are more and more popular. Radios and recordings have long since left once hallowed places in living rooms and moved in vast numbers into bedrooms and bathrooms, bars and barber shops, offices, hotel lobbies, automobiles, and ball parks; pocket-size transistors are everywhere, indoors and out. The quality of ubiquitousness enables what one media reseacher calls "angelization—the quality of having one's spirit freed from flesh, capable of instant transportation anywhere."[25]

Underlying this growth of all media is the fact, borne out in various studies, that the more time one spends with any medium, the more likely he is to pay attention to a number of others. While conversation of persons who are aware of media often centers on their experiences and may also be characterized by more breadth, they are consistent in the type of medium observed. Also, the person who reads confession magazines will prefer radio and television's soap opera and popular recordings and will probably purchase romantic mass-market paperback fiction and attend movies with similar content.

Content rests in a flat sealed can, with darkness inside, until the lid is removed and replaced with the filter of the mass media. For example, the report of the National Advisory Commission on Civil Disorders in 1968 contained a strong condemnation of American racial separatism. In paperback form, it became an overnight bestseller. A journalist observed that most people received their impressions of the report as it was filtered through newspapers, television and magazines.[26] One medium vied with another to edit the content for maximum marketability.

The media themselves are aware of their own power to slant, as well as the fact that they are also forced to make decisions involving editorial judgment. The release of President Nixon's Watergate transcript of 240,000 words afforded an unprecedented challenge for them to exercise their judgment, as well as an opportunity to compete with each other in speed and manner of presentation. *Newsweek* magazine recounts the varied ways in which varied media jumped to meet the challenge.[27] News people in record numbers scrambled to Washington to work all night in order to obtain excerpts for the morning papers. The Memphis *Commercial Appeal* urged readers to buy the 1,308 page version for $12.25 from the Government Printing Office. It sold out its 800-copy first edition in three hours. The *Chicago Tribune* included the transcript as a supplement to its regular issues; other newspapers ran it in a series. Three major television networks devoted lavish amounts of time to the original as well as to the commentary. National Public Radio held a marathon reading of the entire transcript over its 164 stations. Several paperback publishers—Dell, Bantam, and Macmillan—rolled their presses at once with sale price editions costing $10.95 and up.

Aware of the impact of sensory appeal, producers in all media vie with each other for vividness, drama and dynamism of presentation. They enable people to fill a basic desire—that of being in two places at the same time or in several places in rapid succession. On the weekend of November 22, 1963, for example, an entire generation of Americans was jerked from a muffled drum corps and a grim caisson moving up Pennsylvania Avenue in Washington, D.C. to a gunshot in a dingy, jammed police station in Dallas.

The visual emphasis of television and the movies has contributed to the "picturizing" effect on all media; even the audial media of radio and recordings try to show their messages. These "beefed up" ersatz images help sustain our harried existence. The response of people in their real environment may well be to a media-controlled "picture of the world" to which they have been exposed constantly all their lives.

Any student or citizen fond of records or television or magazines has little reason to complain to teachers that they should "tell it like it is, man." If he does, he shows great ignorance of the distortion by the mass media. The recording, television, and film industries have hundreds of techniques for manipulating the human voice; drafting, photography and printing can be manipulated to achieve a specific result. And the content is so persuasively contrived and routine as to make people believe that formulas and themes and stereotypes are the way things actually were or are.

The sensory metaphors have become fully mixed. Photography has provided the foundation for the new kinds of pictorial and trick realism. A page of comics or cartoons speaks ten thousand words, more or less, and no one asks why.[28] Picture books and magazines abound, since more people can see than can read, and many people find reading a hindrance to perception and appreciation. The paperback edition appears to some more digestible than the hard cover. The audience responsiveness to this picture age and the capsulation trend is almost terrifying in its scope and development.

CRISIS OR POTENTIAL?

Pictorial emphasis and an attempt at mass appeal often make the communications content seem vulgar, sensational, crass, and even sordid. One is reminded of Pitrim Sorokin's summing up of contemporary art as "primarily a museum of social and cultural pathology. It centers in the police morgue, the criminal's hide-out, and the sex organs, operating mainly on the level of the social sewers."[29] Frequently this content promises quick relief, inevitable results, and rich rewards for its communicator. It capitalizes on poverty, dissatisfaction, unrest, ignorance, irresponsibility, insecurity and fear. Sheer emotional stimulation flourishes through the press, radio and television; from there, unfortunately, it penetrates the elementary and secondary schools, as well as institutions of higher learning.

Traditionally, after completion of formal schooling, the average youth was supposed to be capable of understanding the mores of the community, and weighing intelligently its good and its evil aspects. But the twentieth century has thrust an overwhelming quantity of demands relating to morals, ethics and intelligence upon an untutored person before and during school years and for the rest of his life. Observing this constant daily bombardment of news, entertainment, and announcements, H. A. Overstreet affirmed: "It is more than likely that we might properly be called newspaper-made, radio-made, movie-made and advertisement-made people."[30]

Beware, say many concerned citizens, lest dishonesty, bribery and selfishness be courted by the communicator and his content be a fraud and a threat to human well-being.

Many of the denunciations of mass media are indicative of a conflict in tastes between relatively small audiences of people who claim to have "high culture" and a vast majority of other Americans whose culture "runs to different things: to ball games rather than art museums, to popular songs rather than symphonies, to swiftly-told action drama rather than subtle studies of character," according to Frank Stanton, President of Columbia Broadcasting Corporation.[31] He recalled the class-conscious attitude that James Boswell reported in an eighteenth-century drawing room: a gentleman maintained that the art of printing had hurt real learning by disseminating idle writing and that a general diffusion of knowledge among a people made the vulgar rise above their humble sphere. Others in history, both governors and governed, have viewed learning as a curse and printing as a dangerous device; they have prayed: "God keep us from both."

We cannot afford such exclusiveness. Today's people, the ruling and the ruled, must note that if a mass medium ceases to reflect the diverse interests of the society it serves, or if it aims to please only a single, even if high, level of taste, it is no longer one of the vital links of modern society. No less emphatically, they must note that educators have an obligation constantly to raise the popular level of tastes. As Professor Moses Hadas declared in his book, *Old Wine, New Bottles,* "The knightly ideal is no longer restricted to knights, but has been made accessible to every man— or better, every man is now a knight. That is the essential value of democracy."[32]

Whenever any one medium is so dominant as to attract repeatedly brazen, sensation-seeking or self-centered charlatans who dwell on the demon in people, and to repel meek, modest and altruistic personalities who would bring out the angel in people, there is justification for reproach. At the same time, suspicion or blame laid on any mass medium is unfair if it overlooks the fact that film, tape, disc, cable, print or wave are in themselves neutral. They can transmit the good as readily as the shoddy, the superior as readily as the mediocre, the challenging as well as the boring. Merely using a medium is neither to the credit nor the discredit of the medium itself.

The intense simultaneity of "blaring radios and Musak and blaring-glaring television," according to English professor James Smith, results in a deconcentrated, or unconcentrated state of mind, leaving it to take in nothing at all. The antennae are deactivated.[33] In a related sense, the mind becomes a mere assembly line for externally induced thoughts. Sociologists describe a "narcotizing dysfunction." They say that the media pump into the human brain an unending stream of information, opinion, moral values and aesthetic taste, which neutralizes the audiences into a mechanical response. A pediatrician, T. Berry Brazelton, noted that the older a child gets, the easier it is for him to get "hooked" on medium exposure, for he loses his power to tune out or tune in visual and auditory cues.[34]

The danger seen by David Sarnoff, Chairman of the Radio Corporation of America, is that the habit of endless change may be carried over into departments of life that rest on principles that are changeless. "And it is precisely this danger that men and their institutions of education must consciously guard against," he has written.[35] The potential for a mass medium to magnify value changes, whether corrupt or upright or nil, requires the very highest integrity of the communicators. It demands the best professional advice and leadership and creative talent from devoted educators and their students and associates. Together, they must understand the new revolutionary dynamism of the media and help to cage the tiger.

Without the educator, public communicators may drag the minds of people through a never-ending series of changes, some as convulsive as a violent revolution. Any communicator can reign like a king over the millions who make up his great audiences, but as soon as the season changes, he may be merely a cabbage-head slated for the compost heap. The educator and communicator must assist in assuring continuity and sanity in guiding the revolution to purposeful ends.

The immediate question may well be whether guidance is ever possible while the revolution continues. Can the mass media revolutionary takeover be slowed down long enough to affect a working courtship, if not a marriage, with public education? As Douglas Cater, Director of the Aspen Program on Communications and Society, stated: "The output of our media is increasingly recognized as integral to the education process and more fundamental to a free society than formal schooling. Yet we sadly lack the sound base of research and analysis with which to measure the media's role and to design our communication's future."[36] Herbert Schiller, writing on communications and technology, stated: "Failure to reshape domestic and environmental adaptability can only deepen the disorders already wracking American society."[37]

To an audience of public administrators, former White House Press Secretary Pierre Salinger phrased the dilemma this way: "Perhaps in the long run, we will find that the communications revolution has run away from us and that we have neither the ability nor the desire to adjust life and our practices to meet the problems with which it has presented us." Should this happen, Salinger concluded, society "will ride from crisis to crisis, from crest to crest of 'happenings,' many of which are completely fabricated to give people access to the media, because they will find that is the only way left for them to communicate."[38]

Techniques for reaching out to greater audiences are being perfected at a much faster pace than ever dreamed when the first telegraph message was sent from Maine to Texas. Thoreau warned against the danger, lest the techniques be only a pretty toy, an improved means to an unimproved end, distracting our attention from serious things.[39] There might be nothing important to communicate. The nineteenth-century social critic Thomas Carlyle seems to have been left cold concerning the communications prospects of rapidly developing technology. When informed of the completion of the England-to-India undersea telegraph cable, he is said to have asked: "Oh? What do we have to say to India?"

One observer, Brenda Maddox, calls present-day communications a "liberating technology," and says fears of it are grossly exaggerated. It offers a crowded planet a sense of community and the benefits of paneled intelligence. "It is possible to retard technological change," she adds, "but in communications it would be wrong."[40] More specifically, the critical need is media application and direction for the benefit of mankind and its civilization.

4

A REVOLUTION TOO MILD – EDUCATION

Mass public education, like mass public communications, has not only undergone periodic change but has also become an instrument for dramatic change throughout society. Leaders of government coups continue to use education as a means of political indoctrination. Once at the helm, a dictator, with deep confidence in the power of education, quickly forms a state monopoly to insure its dedication to his interests. More often than not, he neglects to assess whether his actions are more convulsive than constructive.

In endless succession, the ordinary entertainers, commentators and heroes created and stylized for people who are regarded as the masses strut their stuff on television or radio, in films or recordings, or in print. They spark quick revolutions in desire, taste, attitude, interest and fashion. Claiming to march with a banner of educational improvement, some students and faculty members become media-enveloped to the point of confusing their campus purpose with unrest, revolt, and even dictatorship of personal demands. But the strutting and marching seldom last longer than a few seasons, and the action generated is just as temporary.

The truly educated person has been and always must be in the forefront of people's permanent leadership for action. His is a steady contribution of worthy and lasting merit, an attempt to defy the words of the Italian dictator Mussolini: "There is no revolution which can change the nature of man."

On the other hand, educators have a clear and valid direction, they can help people to change themselves. Were educators also to clarify their progressive goals and then to share them with the communication in-dustry, the changes could be truly revolutionary. As philosopher Ortega y Gasset noted, true revolution is more like a state of mind than a series of convulsions.[1] It is not accurately or appropriately reflected in a narrative of the terrifying aspects of modern technology, such as is implied in Alan Toffler's book, *Future Shock*.[2] In attempting an "anatomy" of revolu-tion, Crane Brinton affirms that it can be a mark of strength and youth-ful soul rather than of error, disorder and decadence.[3] It shows direction.

Writing on the need for revolution in American education, former U.S. Commissioner of Education, Francis Keppel, described three revolu-tions in American education: the first was in quantity and meant that everyone was provided education of some sort; the second was in equality of opportunity, and is still underway; the third, which is still to come, will be a revolution in quality.[4] More abstractly, in their book on *The Re-volution in Education*, Mortimer Adler and Milton Mayer commented: "To the extent that the search for the best education persists, the search for the best society persists, and in the measure that the best education is achieved will the best society be achieved."[5] The most important revolu-tion, the one that will improve the quality of education, and thus of American life, is slow in coming.

CHANGES IN THE EDUCATIONAL SCENE

Even though there is much to be done, vast strides have been made over the last decades. The little red schoolhouse that contained several grades was a familiar sight during the first half of the 20th century in many places. Often it was on the edge of town, and its playground doubled as cow pasture. Within a few decades, it was replaced by magni-ficent centers for art, health, literature, music, science, administration, re-creation and food services. A simple frame building yielded to a complex of bright and airy structures of steel and glass.

An equally dynamic growth is characteristic of high schools and col-leges, in both small towns and large cities. The campus of the late 1960s witnessed a major building boom throughout the country. Classrooms have been enlarged, modernized and mechanized. Youth move in a pleasant and often plush atmosphere of highly planned and stimulating learning centers. A wide array of teaching accessories and gadgets is at hand. The gigantic expansion in facilities for both academic and non-academic needs was designed to accommodate a large increase of student enrollments within two decades. The sizes of faculties have similarly increased.

The size and quality of instructional faculties have increased. The teacher is better prepared. Much more is known today than ever before on how and what teachers should teach. The old normal school, which educated so many teachers, has vanished, and teacher-preparation curricula have been broadened to include a substantial number of liberal arts courses. Enrollments in colleges of education sagged during the 1970s, as they did in all academic areas, but countless numbers of young people still look forward to a career in teaching.

Changes have also been numerous in the variety of institutions, their system of government, the organization of their faculties and student bodies, their curricular offerings and the functions of testing, counseling, research and public service. Education has advanced with revolutionary strides to become a huge business and a powerful profession. Legislatures and foundations have engineered dramatic programs to enable every high school graduate to attend college. State and federal scholarship programs, guaranteed loans, work-study arrangements, and projects for the disadvantaged insure that no individual will be kept from the campus because of economic reasons.

The world, however, neither stands still nor waits until all young citizens receive their college degrees. Some youth rebel because the diplomas lose their hoped-for meaning almost at once. They leave college little able to face the outside world. Their buying power is less than anticipated. They are confronted by a rapidly changing population, with new competitions from racial minorities and women, with new regard for the aging. Limitations on natural resources, the search for new arteries of power, and extensions of speed and space confuse the picture further. Education, it turns out, proves to do little to help them cope with this revolutionary environment.

It is catastrophic that the campus image that spread across the newspapers was for several years one of rebellion and confrontation. At the end of the 1960s, radical individuals and organizations brought to a climax a progression of activism from "Freedom Now!" (1960) and "Power Now!" (1964) to "Revolution Now!" (1968) that made many campuses a center of property destruction and killing.[6] Stimulated by noncampus forces that objected to the Establishment's slow resolution of social and environmental problems and the persistence of the Vietnam War, these forces took every advantage of instant communications that the media made available. Spokesmen for organizations such as Students for a Democratic Society (SDS) proclaimed an unequivocal goal: to destroy the universities by cutting the lines of communication and to conspire to annihilate the trust upon which universities are built. Perhaps no more mortal blow could be conceived, for, as was written in the *Chicago Daily News*, at stake was a "trust in one another, trust in learning, trust in reason."[7]

The campus was stunned into ineffectiveness, and when the riots faded, they left disbelief and apathy in their wake. In any long-range evaluation, however, the rebels will prove to have been mere convulsions, not at all to be confused with significant revolutionary values in education or communication.

In size and scope, the campus has been called an uncontrollable giant; it is clumsy, backward and slothful. Departments and other organizational units have become extremely independent, and the extremism mounts. Logan Wilson, former Director of the American Council on Education, referred to campuses as an agglomeration of entities connected only by a common plumbing system.[8] Under the guise of innovative purpose, the patterns of education, the institutional rearrangements, cooperative consortia, state systems, and government grants often remain without basic change in content. Any modicum of revolutionary substance usually remains isolated, if not completely dissipated.

Reasons for the lag in educational change are cited by both professional and laymen. Many state that education is too decentralized, its organization and structure too loose, the training of teachers wholly inadequate and the compensation too meager. Some educators draw a comparison with the strong organization, extensive training and high salaries of the physicians and dentists. Others envy the powerful unions and the subsequent bargaining power and the high wages of tradesmen in occupations requiring little formal education. Contradictory and confusing views such as these make the system appear awkward, inefficient, and unproductive, as well as unable to change itself. They help to explain a conservative reaction in the 1970s throughout society.

EDUCATION'S LEADING TASK

Such criticisms rarely manage to confront the cause of the central problem, but rather, they tend to examine the symptoms. Most critics fail to examine the overall purpose of the system, the structure that must change if education is to survive. Is the educational revolution too slow or too narrow in scope? What is unique about the function or objective of education in today's world? How should the educator fulfill this function? How effective can he be?

Educators have asked these questions for many years in speeches and in documents. The pace of their discussion has sped up in recent decades. The constructive controversies their questions raise are in themselves indicative of the revolution that is under way.

Some questions of a more specific nature are also in more critical need of satisfactory response. Should educational enrichment be largely for the intellectually elite and gifted or is it more important for persons of average intelligence and willingness to learn? Is there a definable body of facts, truths and values that every citizen ought to know? What is the professional educator's responsibility for the myriad of educating and de-educating forces outside the classroom? Firm and unequivocal answers to these questions would be a proof of true educational potential. Such answers as exist still lie with liberal-general education transmitted in the classroom and exhibited outside the classroom through cooperation with the public mass media.

Modern society thrives on a multitude of complementary and interlocking trades and professions acquired under disparate curricula. Vocational specialization has become so profound as to cause awesome differences among persons. How little the atomic engineer or the mortality statistician can know about ophthalmology or medieval archives! Vocational variations in themselves, however, contribute nothing toward bringing together individuals within a society.

Rather, the sense of wholeness of a modern society is brought about through an extensive common fund of operational knowledge, conceptions, principles and values. Individuals draw from this fund to identify, interpret, select and build into their own lives the components of a cultural heritage that leads to richer understanding of and participation in the world today.

Several agencies formulate and transmit this knowledge to members of society. The home, the church, the library, the museum, the playground, the peer groups, social and political associations, trade and professional organizations and the mass media all help to teach people what they must know to survive in their environment. But from none is more expected than from the college and university; their chief weapon in this time of specialization is liberal and general education.

Elaborate distinction between liberal and general education is of secondary importance here, although a discussion of differences may be helpful. Their largely common purpose and content are the essential concern. Two college presidents, writing several years ago, said that everyone needs "general education first, to make men feel at home in the physical, social and intellectual world; then liberal education to bring out the pattern of his individuality, to prepare him for responsible leadership; and finally specialized or professional education to induce the skills by which he can make a living."[9]

Many use the two terms interchangeably. A 1947 report of the President's Commission on Higher Education states that "the two differ mainly in degree, not in kind. General education undertakes to redefine liberal education in terms of life's problems as men face them, to give it human orientation and social direction, to invest it with content that is directly relevant to the demands of contemporary society . . . . General education is liberal education with its matter and method shifted from its original aristocratic intent to the service of democracy. General education seeks to extend to all men the benefits of an education that liberates."[10]

As mentioned earlier, the differences are inconsequential for purposes of this discussion; however, of central importance is the recognition that liberal-general education is needed by all citizens who are to be effective, regardless of their profession or trade. The citizen needs an appreciation of world cultures and of the significant accomplishments and unfinished business of civilization. He must be helped to develop a keen and ready understanding, intuition and imagination. He must acquire the arts of discriminating between good and bad, and he must learn to make decisions with temperance and magnanimity. His philosophy of thought and action must be responsible and productive. Modern society requires the citizen-student to think, to relate, to reason, and to evaluate—all against a background of appropriate standards of conduct, discipline and values.

The scope of such education necessarily embraces the entire world in which people live. In curricular terms, knowledge of this world involves knowledge of the languages, literature, philosophies, mathematics, social studies and natural and physical sciences. They impel the student ever to learn more: to review the past, observe the present and foresee the future; to seek and to discover the best there is to know and do.

Waves of criticism and complaint recur about liberal arts and general studies programs in college and high school. Indicative of the mood of many people in the early 1970s was the frank statement of Columbia University Professor Jacques Barzun: "The liberal arts tradition is dead or dying."[11] At the same time, such long-time defenders as Robert Hutchins and Mortimer Adler were quoted by those businessmen who have remained believers in the intelligence, literacy and adaptability the liberal arts courses offer. Similarly, a national journal for public administrators lauds the broad perspective of "a first-class liberal arts education or its equivalent" as a necessary prerequisite for men and women who will become leaders in public life.[12] Wherever the media industries have prescribed the best kind of training for entry into their profession, they have stressed the importance of basic courses of study in the social sciences, natural sciences and humanities.

While modifications in a liberal-general program are inevitable, no educator can deny the need for a broad approach to equip the specialist to relate his work to other human endeavors. Students are up in arms against unimaginative, specialized teaching, the loss of faith by teachers and administrators, and the absence of their honest example of intellectual liberation. As lifelessly as the classroom content is often presented, the serious student and teacher have found no substitute for knowledge that reflects both breadth and depth.

Contrary to the claims of some critics, the promotion of liberal arts and general education is not an attempt to prolong what some consider defunct movements in educational history; nor is it a question of pressing to retain outmoded methodology or taxonomy. Rather, the promotion reflects the need to keep all channels of knowledge exchange open and to cultivate a means of organizing the exchange to make it easier to teach and to learn. A framework of liberal-general studies helps the acquaintanceship with many great minds and with the informational outputs of the computer. It fosters liberation from both superiority and inferiority, from vanity, prejudice, vulgarity and cruelty.

Catherine Marshall, author of *A Man Called Peter*, has called for a return to the great heritage of the liberal arts—"that of the maturation of the whole man and woman; to become once again the fountainhead of daringly creative leadership; to wrest from the yellow press and the commercialism of TV and the movies the prerogative of being progenitor and custodian of the nation's ideas and ideals. In so doing our colleges and universities might once again become the cradle of the soul of a nation."[13] Does her statement not suggest that a first step might be for the educator to turn toward, not from, the press, television and movies?

Notre Dame University President Theodore M. Hesburgh stated: "Only liberal education proposes to teach a man what he is and can be, what he has been and why. Only liberal education can give a unified overview of the world and man, of values, ultimate goals, and the broad truths that apply to every kind of human activity and guide every human aspiration."[14] What will be necessary, educators ask, for this great directive and inspirational force to live up to its promise, or even to survive as a beacon in the darkness?

THE REVOLUTION FALTERS

In the 1960s many regarded the revolution in education as too mild because teaching procedures were resistant to change, innovation and improvement. This resistance, President Alvin Eurich of the Fund for the Advancement of Education laid to tradition, laziness, comfort, economy, technology and lack of interest.[15] The hope offered by a liberal-general curriculum has always been shackled by such barriers as vested interest, habit, inertia, a failure of the nerve of leadership and parochialism that bind it from within. Anti-intellectualism and ignorance hobble it from without. Despite the innovations of education and the feeling that change might indeed be occurring, the inhibitions of education appear to remain painfully unchanged over the decades.

For instance, educators have long arbitrarily compelled students .to perform during the "traditional" school year. It is the period of nine months of instruction followed by a three-month period when students take vacation or other diversion and teachers are expected to improve (or restore) themselves intellectually. The school year is normally split into semesters or quarters, which, in turn, are further interrupted by Christmas and spring holidays. If family or occupational obligations or personal illness interfere, a setback results, and the student must await the beginning of a new term. This conformist schedule often discourages persons from continuous and intensive application to study.

The tradition of four years in high school, followed by a minimum of two or four years in college is a hindrance for the serious learner, that has long been called an "academic lockstep."[16] One's disposition, intelligence and freedom from entangling occupational or familial obligations may not coincide with the stringent time frame. One begins to feel that intellectual accomplishment is quite secondary to the four years of "residence" required in the case of a baccalaureate degree. To gauge the work of students by an arbitrary measure of time is to delay many from beginning advanced work and to compel others to do hurried and poor work. While a few public and private high schools have attempted to meet the problem in part, often with prodding from government funding, the concessions have been slow and fraught with controversy.

Some of the blame for the failure of general-liberal education to improve itself must also fall on a misplaced emphasis on textbooks. As new instructional aids are needed, educators often are tempted by immediate financial profit and social or professional prestige to write and market textbooks or programmed learning booklets that are less than educationally sound. Either inadvertently or deliberately, some instructors limit their teaching efforts to a rigidly determined batch of textbooks or programs that students need only memorize and parrot back on examinations. The result is even worse when the curricular content comes solely from a set of lecture notes that are little revised from year to year.

Liberal and general education's potential is thus placed in jeopardy. Exploration of other fields of learning is viewed with pity or disdain. Query is received with indifference, and dissent with disapproval. Independent interpretation, without the authority of expert vision or a citation, is viewed with suspicion. The sharp lines and tight compartments of specialized knowledge become neatly constructed in students' minds. The more years they attend college, the more they become specialists and the more they fear unsound generalization, especially about the contemporary and the unauthenticated.

Heavy emphasis on textbooks, lectures and examinations tends inevitably to hold the student in a captive world that is neither his own nor commensurate with his potential. The purely methodological criteria are used to sift out the contemporary intellectual substance, the spiritual excellence and the social relevance that stimulate students. Cultivation of only one of a few functions of the mind in a framework of restrictions leaves a life that is unbalanced and stifled. The goal will more than likely be merely to earn the necessary credits for graduation, rather than to seek an education. As William S. Learned wrote in the 1930s, the educational experience has become a matter of credits *versus* education,[17] rather than credits toward education.

Some educators and educational supporters have stifled the potential of liberal-general education by various forms of vocationalism without having assessed whether it is apt to be irrelevant or unnecessary for the student. Preparation in high school or college for specialized technical or professional occupations when only 15 or 20 percent of the labor force can absorb graduates in these areas is folly. Moreover, when a technological shift sharply changes the demand for persons trained in certain highly specialized roles, the consequence is further disillusionment over education. During the race to explore outer space, for example, the United States government supported an almost fanatical drive to recruit and train nuclear physicists and technicians; within a few short years thousands of them were pumping gas or engaged in other jobs far removed from their training. College graduates who confuse job training with liberal-general education sooner or later will discover they have been betrayed into narrowness.

Some educators put hobbles on liberal-general education through parochialism. A general studies and liberal arts program should be a preparation for thinking. It is basically intellectual. But the intellect cannot function in a vacuum. Actual experiences and problems of life are all about us. A teacher is remiss if he or she overlooks the many, varied out-of-school activities as instruments of education. Maurice L. Jacks, of the English school system, revealed two derogatory implications of these activities: they are out-of-school, and it is in school that education takes place; they are "activities" in presumed contradiction to the "passivity" of the classroom.[18]

As a natural result of ignoring outside experiences, Joseph K. Hart has pointed out that school has become something to be escaped from by most alert children and youth in order that their real education may proceed.[19] Liberal arts students participating in a study by the Center for Research and Development in Higher Education noted a systematic inflexibility, "a confining grind," and "a deadly rerouting" that forced them to abandon their pursuit of self-knowledge and creative interests.[20] Harvard College students have sometimes been stereotyped as preferring a "gentleman's C" for a grade in order to enjoy the broad experiences of life.

A related failing, which can partly be attributed to the parochialism of teaching and the overdepartmentalism of subject areas, is the inability of most students to combine learning and leisure. It is a pernicious doctrine that splits up an individual's life into unharmonized parts of curriculum and recreation. The system of academic credits and grade-point awards leaves leisurely pursuits in a secondary position. The drive for academic achievement is unconducive to study that is leisurely or recreational. Study and learning are hard work; except for the very few, often labeled "grinds," study and pleasure do not mix. In a manner destructive to the ideas of liberal-general education, a barrier between two worlds of learning and leisure persists into the adult years.

In the face of the many problems of education, a continual bustle of concern, study and reporting is underway by the professional leadership. Educational associations and commercial firms distribute countless pieces of literature and hold hundreds of conferences with such themes as "How to Get and Keep Members," "How to Raise Funds," and "How to Pressure the Lawmakers." The media contacts are largely limited to use of a manual such as "How to be Heard; Making the Media Work for You," and the maintenance of public relations, fund raising and image-building machinery.[21] All of the fanfare seems to be limited to the promotion of a single level, product, service or section of an organization. Where in all of the flurry can one find a modicum of serious, penetrating analysis of educational aims and content? Where is the woefully needed concern with the development of *all* of the people as a primary objective of education?

In summary, the main reason for the failure of education to revolutionize more rapidly is largely narrow vision. The broad range of acculturizing and educational influences remains out of view. Anti-intellectualism sets in simply because the stress is upon pursuing a vocation and a specialty, even though it may have intellectual substance. The vision falls short of guiding individuals into becoming intelligent and productive citizens, participants in the cultivation of human values and virtues that are by nature broad rather than narrow. Anti-educator sentiment grows when, to paraphrase a statement by Newton and Nell Minow, "the last group to understand how to use the media has been professional educators."[22] The pursuit of academic fullness and excellence lacks meaning; the present suffers, and the future can be no better.

THE LARGER CULTURE AND THE LARGER AUDIENCE

Much of the disappointment over education lies in some of its oft-repeated promises. On reading a typical description of a curriculum in a college catalogue, one may be led to believe that it provides the greatest possible breadth of valuable experience. On hearing the speeches of education promoters, both in and out of politics, one may still feel that anyone without at least two years on a college campus soon might or should be an oddity among citizens fully prepared for life. The views of these people misinterpret the honest claims made with regard to the true purpose of colleges and universities, as well as of precollegiate schooling.

In his book, *The Aims of Education and Other Essays*, philosopher Alfred North Whitehead stated, "There is only one subject-matter for education, and that is Life in all its manifestations."[23] Numerous other educators have expressed much the same idea in noting that nature, civic conditions, the street, travel, beauty and ugliness, fortunes and misfortunes, punishments and rewards, work and play all educate the people. In fact, it is said, whatever touches people educates them if they respond in any way to it.

It should be stressed that education is the bridge to the transmission of culture from one generation to another. Sociologists call this process "acculturization." Daily human relationships contribute to the process by shaping behavior and thinking into socially productive patterns. Clergymen and statesmen incline people toward worthy religious and political aspirations. And on the shoulders of educators rests the chief responsibility for coordination and leadership in transmitting and improving the culture as a whole. In this respected and valid task, professional education is milling around and dragging its feet. Lawmakers are among those who say it is stagnating. Educational change has been overtaken by the revolution of the modern mass media of public communications. Further, as if second place in the race to complete its own objectives were not serious or ludicrous enough, formal education has been slow to recognize the educational benefits of the public mass media. Finally, the educational establishment continues to be hesitant and even afraid to define and counteract the educationally detrimental influences of the media.

Educators have given considerable attention to the teaching of critical acumen in the reading of selected, largely hard-cover books. They have avoided many attempts to cultivate a critical eye for the other media. Writing about humanists and the mass media, Paul L. MacKendrick expressed disappointment that the education of critical taste in films has seemed unworthy of educator attention. At the same time, he noted that little contact with books is apt to be maintained after formal schooling has ended "while commercial films, like the poor, are always with us."[24]

In the study of the mass media as communicators of culture, formal education has fallen especially short. Where does the classroom teach about that part of life that includes the commercials on radio and television and the advertisements in magazines for cola drinks and toothpaste, cigarettes and beer, floor wax and home permanents, deodorants and insurance? What comments emanate from the classroom on sports, comics, or cartoons? On the Westerns and mysteries? On the ten thousand violent acts per television weekend? What about the crooners, rock-and-rollers, frugers and twisters, or their faddist ballroom successors?. Preposterous questions, one may say, for certainly these are not educational. Yet, these are all part of life. Perhaps Whitehead was in error, and education is not life written so large. More accurately, while meaningful education is broadening, it is also selective as it confronts the totality of life. In any case, for many persons, answers to these questions fall with a thud, for they appear to accentuate the slow pace and an ever-narrowing scope of the educational revolution. As far as most of the population is concerned, campus education is a tortoise that has less than a fable's chance of winning the race with the hare that is the mass media.

"Though the world is in transition to a post-industrial society," an article in *Media and Methods* reports, "our school systems are still busy preparing for a nineteenth century industrial world."[25] The subjects that are taught have changed little in the span of fifty years. Moreover, another critical article maintains, they are failing to meet the democratic challenge of caring for the poor and dispossessed, and they are harboring "positively destructive influences for many of the children entrusted to their care."[26]

Among American adults, only a very small proportion engage in formal education. Americans all, by far most of them, live a life of the barest exposure to the organized and seasoned offerings of formal education and its edifice of curricula. Most of them patronize and even worship almost anything at other altars, including the disorganization and de-education readily and freely set before them by the all-inclusive mass media. For millions, classroom education is death and educators are deadheads, while jukeboxes, television, movies, radio, comic books, paperbacks and picture magazines beat out the lively pulse of life. In contrast to dull-appearing teachers of artificial subjects, the crooners, columnists and comedians of media content seem sparklingly alive, even though they may not always present a desirable side of life. The ways of "civilization," as seen through the media, are not those of the educator and the idealist, but rather, are those of the merchant and the materialist. The exploitation of crime and sensuality largely reflect the minds of profiteers and sadists on the subjects of human well-being.

Public Patience

Ironically, the public view of education as dull and slow has produced little reaction. Declining enrollment may be a symptom of the disillusionment by society, but it is also considered to be the result of population changes. The majority of young people still submit to high school and even college courses without seriously questioning their value. Citizens and taxpayers in general still support the educational institutions because they prefer to believe that education is basically a good cause.

Today's educated person feels the need of a badge to display, a sheepskin to frame, and a shingle to hang, all of which announce that he is an informed, liberated and inspired person. He still conceives of education as the unique key for unlocking the doors of information and culture. Young people are told by their peers and elders that education is a quantitative right. Had our founding fathers seen education as institutionalized as it became in the twentieth century and as universally supported as it became in the early 1960s, they might well have expanded the phrase in the Declaration of Independence to "Life, Liberty, and the pursuit of Happiness and Education."

Educators know, at least in principle, what their profession should accomplish: everyone must be made aware of and conversant with his or her cultural heritage, the facts of the sciences, and the rules of acceptable individual and social behavior. Everyone must seek and find the skill to meet wisely the problems that he will encounter during his life. It is unfortunate when attitudes for liberalizing and broadening are thwarted by forcing the college student, and the high school student as well, to choose a field of concentration or to make a vocational commitment whether or not he is ready for it.

Guidance in meeting these problems is with awesome frequency limited to a few remarks at the opening of the academic year and at commencement. If a student misses these, it is unlikely that he will have read a statement on objectives, such as is given in a college catalogue, or that he will have read any of the various books or articles on the value of a broadening education. The media claim as one of their functions the task of enlightening the millions that make up the viewing and reading public. But if the public has no inclination to be enlightened, such claims are fallacious and are easily relegated to commercial exploitation. It is the schools that have traditionally planted the prior inclination to be enlightened on many subjects, including those completely unrelated to a job or a paycheck. It is in this way alone that the schools lead in launching any permanent revolution for public responsibility.

In practice, however, the average educator has little sense of urgency to articulate the true purpose of education. He frequently promotes his security rather than his cause. The views reported to a dean or a principal have run something like these: "I don't care who hears my teaching or what my pupils learn." "I don't care if they learn anything." "I'll teach when I'm not occupied with research or writing." "It is up to the pupils to learn. Let the parents take more of the job!" "Teaching, especially in college, is mostly the giving out of grades."

When, on the eve of the 1970s, the practice of student evaluation of teachers spread, grading turned deferential and manipulative, teaching in effect became a consumer service, and popularity as judged by departmental committees ruled as the criterion for teacher merit. Can there be any doubt as to the harm of these kinds of attitudes and assessment, even when they are not expressed and only implied?

The immense public confidence and monetary support for the educational profession weakened immeasurably as the 1960s ended. Funds ran short. Priorities needed a reordering. The public began to question the charge given to professional educators to educate everyone. Could it be that the responsibility was misdirected? The promises to bring the benefits and wonders of liberal and general education to everyone were not being fulfilled. The public lost patience with the capacity of educators to change people for the better. People who do not share in the knowledge and wisdom of the liberally educated will yield to the illiteracy and mental blindness of media addiction. If education ceases to kindle the urge to learn and to disseminate knowledge widely, the mass media will feed on the resulting explosion of ignorance and on human exploitation through propaganda.

Far more widely than a campus curriculum has succeeded in doing, the movies, radio, magazines and newspapers have adapted themselves to the public, as a Harvard University general education report affirmed in the mid-1940s.[27] Have educators, nearing the year 2000, then been asking whether mass media gain is education's loss? Out of pride, indifference, or neglect, has the educator permitted a development in public communications that has resulted in a void into which undesirable elements have entered and become permanently lodged?

The situation between public educator and public communicator is not unlike two rival contenders for political power. The office they seek aims for the attention of the people. Both have much to offer. Having deeper historical roots, formal education wins many of the first battles, but it circumscribes its fighting zone. Lacking such roots, the mass communicators respect no bounds either of subject matter or of audience; they ride the whirlwinds of a later storm and seek only to win the competition.

The revolution of mass communications is one of enraptured means without intelligible ends; the revolution of higher education is one of passionate ends without efficacious means. For example, about electronic learning, one reads that "This is the first time in which every man everywhere can know what is happening to any man anywhere—instantaneously. This makes it also possible for every man everywhere to know what any other man knows."[28] He has the right "to seek, receive and impart information and ideas through any media and regardless of frontiers."[29] About campus objectives, years of commencement speeches have enjoined us to learn all that we need in order to become all that we should—a vague statement compared to the ones about the media's possibilities. It is little wonder that people in honest pursuit of enlightenment are not only confounded but also disgusted.

The public waits for more than commencement talk and ambivalence. The educator must act. His task is formidable. He must leave the comfort of the ivory tower and leave it as an honest educator dedicated to the love of learning and pursuit of enlightenment. Understanding that millions do not even know who he is and certainly do not receive his message, he must recognize that universal, general-liberal education within the framework of formal instruction is impossible. The cue for the educator is to keep the school facilities and the college aid programs coming, but not to neglect the "real life" media. They, too, are here to stay and for more people and more schedules than the schools can ever accommodate.

An educator cannot accomplish the broad objectives of his profession with antiquated methods and one-sided public relations. He deludes himself, damages his profession and shortchanges his community if he clings tenaciously to anachronistic patterns or joins the chorus for material gain. Accomplishing the ideals of real education, broad culture, and good citizenship for everyone remains a vital goal, but in the world of mass communication, to attempt this effort through schools alone is like using a twig to beat back a hurricane. The educator must use the media.

The American public wants guidance. The educator can respond if he understands, in a classic example, what happened on the day of the assassination of President John F. Kennedy and during the long weekend that followed. At no time in history was so full a measure of liberal-general education concentrated in so brief a period. During the first few hours, radio and television conveyed most of the report, and by late afternoon, the newspapers had reached millions more. The networks announced that their reporters and analysts would stay on the air full time and supplement their coverage with appropriate commentary, as well as with symphonic music and other consonant offerings. Commercials were abandoned. Film clips were available the next day; magazine articles appeared in two or three days, with special issues and paperbacks during the weeks following, carrying detailed analyses.

As the *Columbia Journalism Review* noted, "the occurrences of November 22 to 25, 1963 belonged to journalism," as it tried "to feed a hunger that, for once, could not be satisfied—for information, for explanation, for reassurance."[30] This time, for however brief a period, the mainstream of relevant educational content flowed to the people almost exclusively in a unified manner through the mass media.

It was clear that the role of educators was a tributary to the main-stream. Administrative staffs, faculty and students at colleges and univer-sities, as well as in high schools, found their usual endeavors pointless. Media people saw little need to call in educators who could do little more than conduct a small memorial service of their own. The nation's cam-puses—the very center for educational responsibility and service—seemed unable to do more than to close for a day of tribute. Stunned by their help-less condition and perhaps also resentful of the educational success of an-other social institution, they never gave the media due acknowledgement for an educational task well performed.

The dramatic weekend of intense historical drama leaves unans-wered questions. If mass media can react in such a way at a time of na-tional crisis, does the public not have a right to expect them to raise their level of performance on other occasions? More important, if the media can be used in this responsible way, should not educators awaken to the possibilities of being partners in a common cause? Does not the Ameri-can public deserve educational leadership that extends beyond their cam-pus confines?

The revolution in education will come when educators recognize the total framework of mass media—and how it can be used to fulfill educa-tional objectives, when they observe the mass media as channels of educa-tion alongside the long-established channels of home, school, church and state.

It will come when, in their classroom deliberations, educators boldly consider the various media of public communications in homes and meeting halls, at newsstands, on juke boxes, in movie theaters, during tra-vel, and elsewhere. It will come when they wholeheartedly bring the mass media into their teaching, for then they, in turn, find their services in de-mand by those massive forces. A marriage between educators and the media would strengthen the public's faith in education.

The revolutionary development of the public mass media is not going to bring an educational panacea. None of them will ever replace the teacher in face-to-face encounter. But the mass media—all of them—con-tinue their public influence, and the time is long overdue for them to be-come far more effective in offering assistance and cooperation to the teaching profession. Educators, in turn, must recognize the crucial importance of a working liaison so they may gain the mass media as a col-league rather than as a competitor. Division is failure; collaboration can mean triumph. The public waits.

5

TEACHING FOR LEARNING, FORMAL AND INFORMAL

It would be debatable to assert that there is no teaching, only learning, if by such a comment, it is implied that teachers are not necessary or even that learning takes precedence over teaching. It does seem to be without argument, however, to imply that teaching is ineffective unless those being taught have experienced learning.

Oddly enough, a teacher may be an inanimate, impersonal object, event or medium, while a learner is always a human being. The purpose of a teacher or teaching medium is to effect learning, but a learner also has the effect of stimulating teaching. One may say that a teacher cannot teach without learners. People can and do, however, constantly learn from various persons who are not professional teachers, whose educating influence is spread via the mass media rather than being limited to the classroom. At the same time, an understanding of the learning process is a prerequisite to realizing the full promise of effective teaching through mass media.

THE ELEMENTS THAT EDUCATE

How a teacher teaches and how a learner learns are basic questions in the world of education. Conferences and publications of professional associations of education, along with curricula in colleges of education return again and again to these questions. Parents ask how they can help their child to learn and develop more effectively. In the school and the home, as well as in professional education circles, the answers are generally applied to the narrowly restricted formalism of four-walled classrooms.

The belief is widespread that learning first becomes important when a child enters school, and becomes relatively unimportant as soon as a young adult graduates. The teaching process is thought to occur or to be worthy of attention only when practiced by professionally trained, committed, and salaried teachers, and the learning process is thought to exist or to be worthy of attention only in a duly enrolled student. Elsewhere, the two processes are frequently rejected, ignored, or taken for granted.

Our culture has largely neglected the fact that the process of learning may frequently be more significant before and after formal schooling. Because the distinctive presence of a professional teacher is lacking, perhaps the process is less easy to identify during the informal periods of learning. Yet the neglect of informal learning is one of high risk and even of danger, as illustrated by events of violence and unsavory experiences noted in this and other chapters of this book.

Actually, a learner brings his family, neighborhood and social class to a school, as acknowledged in such standard volumes as *The Guidance of Learning Activities* by William Burton.[1] Furthermore, a learner brings the results of learning from a relatively common and uniform exposure to the mass media. In addition to formal classroom instruction for a few hours a day, a few months a year, during childhood and youth, a learner also lives in a milieu of stimuli touching his being during most of the waking hours of every day, month in and month out, during the years before and after formal schooling. Teaching and learning from television, radio, movies, recordings, newspapers, magazines, and paperback books have come to be almost literally omnipresent.

In a very real sense, therefore, the modern mass media must be counted among the most influential teachers in the world. Henry Adams, in his autobiography, says: "A teacher affects eternity; he can never tell where his influence stops."[2] In a similar real sense, the seven "mass media for the millions" (television, radio, movies, etc.) are like the teacher Henry Adams described. They transmit the full gamut of the cultural heritage and shower judgments on every phase of life, period of history and future projection.

Closely allied to the creation of each program and page, disc and tape, is a reporter, author, musician or other performer, advertiser, merchant, manufacturer, propagandist, or preacher—and in fewer cases, a professional teacher. They are endlessly informing, inspiring, comforting, delighting, entertaining, persuading, or selling. For better or for worse, we must recognize, they are also teaching, and the many members of the audiences, persons of all ages, are learning.

The immense educational effect of the mass media becomes ever more impressive when one examines the nature of the learning process. Learning theory, outside professional circles, often seems a hodgepodge of knowledge and conjecture about which there is much disagreement. There is even vociferous lay and semi-professional opinion that learning theory is merely a restatement in technical terms of well-known facts, and, as learning psychologist B. F. Skinner notes in the title of an article, that its very necessity may be questioned.[3] The testimony of other psychologists indicates that theories are admittedly unsettled and often irrelevant.[4]

In particular, in the case of psychologists who devise mazes and models for testing pigeons, dogs, and monkeys under conditions presumed common to all animals, there is the objection that human culture is neither a maze nor a model. Similarly, the outpouring of recorded observation of human learning behavior under controlled and partially controlled conditions should be viewed with a skeptical eye. Undetected variables always exist.[5]

Research shows that learning proceeds most effectively when the learner is motivated by a stake in the activity being undertaken, when the activity involved is geared to the learner's ability, and when he can perceive meaningful progress toward his own goals. Skilled teaching recognizes the importance of an atmosphere conducive to learning, an understanding of when, how, and where the learning challenge should be responded to, and an acceptance of the premise that learning is essentially individual.

Countless personal factors determine the actuality and significance of what is learned, as well as of how and when one learns. Among these are maturation, chronological growth, sex, acquired motives, and developmental potential—all interrelated in different ways and all changing constantly within multifarious settings. These variables converge into a complex of readiness, capacity and inclination that is unique for every person. No less significant than in childhood they seem to come to a focus during high school or college to clinch habits and modes of decisive behavior.

TRANSFER OF LEARNING

Variables affect the way in which learning in one situation is extended into other situations. That this transfer of learning does take place has been shown in numerous experiments on perception, reasoning and other functions. It relies in part on the old and long-respected doctrine of formal discipline: mental faculties of will, memory, attention, judgment, and observation were believed capable of being enlarged and strengthened by continual practice. Thus, subjects such as Latin, Greek and mathematics were considered basic because of their supposed value as instruments for developing the intellect in readiness for learning other subjects.[6]

While this "brain-strengthening" theory no longer enjoys its former stature among psychologists, many educated persons and civic-minded leaders take pride in defending it. Following a campaign speech in 1976, Edmund G. Brown, Jr., Governor of California and candidate for the Democratic presidential nomination, fielded questions from an audience at Johns Hopkins University. In an exchange with an economics professor, he said: "I never took an economics course at college, but I did take eight years of Latin and two years of Greek, which I consider equally relevant to the problems of America."[7]

The basic question, of course, is whether transfer is limited to the "tough subjects." The answer is no. It is more accurate to say that almost *any* learning, regardless of the medium, content, or subject, can be transferred to other learning. For example, the intricacies of football strategy reported in a broadcast or newspaper may have parallels in the mind of a student reading about a battle in European history or attacking a problem in logic.

The potential of learning transfer is naturally more apparent in learning that relates to practical situations and the problems of daily living. Thus the attitudes and behaviors and the facts and ideas communicated by the mass-media becomes generalized into effective influences in subsequent personal situations. The results, indeed, when understood and mastered, become an inseparable part of an outreaching process of learning and education.

Imitation from Repetition

Although stimuli and responses, their selection, interaction and transfer, vary from individual to individual and are subject to other variables, a common characteristic of human behavior is the imitative process.[8] Since the ability to imitate appears early in life, one school of theorists holds it to be instinctive. Another group concludes that imitative behavior is learned through reward and punishment. In its demands for discipline and conformity among its individuals, society trains people to be comfortable (rewarded) when they are doing what others are doing, and miserable (punished) when they are not. Whatever the explanation, imitation of a model is widely acknowledged, making clear the fact that a child learns by example at least as much as by precept.

Imitative behavior follows models set by elders or others and is based on age, social status, intelligence, and skill. Also, certain imitative behavior is expected from certain ages and levels of learning; such terms as "infant," "child," "adolescent," "college student," or "adult" imply the behavior that may be expected and the privileges that may be enjoyed. Increasingly sophisticated behavior symbols serve as stimuli for imitative response. The goal is a world of adult values and behavior patterns, a world portrayed in such expressions as "the way things are," "tell it the way it is," and "let's talk sense." They are the folkways and standards which each new generation inherits—to a large extent through the adult-operated media of public communications, the guidelines for maturity.[9]

The mass media are a potent channel for learning through imitation. The drive to imitate the status, skill, or intelligence of another person may become so powerful as to carry with it a parrotry of mannerisms quite extraneous to the conscious stimulus. For example, an admirer of a movie or television star may copy his or her idol's dress or speech just as a student who is enthusiastic about his or her teacher may adopt some of the teacher's behavioral peculiarities or habits as part of himself or herself.

The sweeping success of the cigarette manufacturers dramatically illustrates the appeal of imitation. Advertisers found that young non-smokers could be counted on to learn smoking if they saw their sports idols, movie heroes, peers and "grown-ups" puffing on cigarettes. For the services of the mass media in teaching the tobacco habit, $200 million a year has not been too much to spend. In 1963 in a concession to critics who saw well the effects of such teaching, the cigarette industry abandoned major advertising in college publications and reiterated that it was not trying to recruit young smokers. In dramatic presentations, talk shows, movies, and comic strips, however, the more subtle yet effective teaching of tobacco use continues.

The Federal Trade Commission followed up on the government report in January, 1964, on the health dangers in smoking, with plans for requiring that all cigarette advertising specify that the habit is hazardous to health. While for some, the impact of an admired model may be weakened, it is unlikely that the small print on cigarette packages or a statement at the end of an advertisement will surmount the learning effect from the repetition of a clever pose or testimonial by an actress, athlete, or executive. The American Cancer Society, among other groups, quickly realized that opposing facts must be presented with equally clever teaching impact for unlearning a habit and for prelearning to prevent the habit. The amplified sound of a heartbeat in danger from smoke inhalation, a picture of soot-coated lungs, and the phrase "It's a matter of life or breath" were combined with presentations of nonsmoking models of good health.

Imitative behavior has become ingrained on the national consciousness. It is witnessed by the fact that every American child recognizes the names of recording stars and cartoon and comic strip characters more easily that those of Plato, Michelangelo, Shakespeare, Kepler, Voltaire, Mozart, Wilson, or Einstein. Moreover, almost all of the latter connote boredom to young people. The first list, surely a product of the mass media, has become the master of our cultural awareness.

Imitation is closely related, for obvious reasons, to repetition. In a long essay on repetition, Kierkegaard asserts that "He who wills repetition is a man, and the more expressly he knows how to make his purpose clear, the deeper he is as a man . . . . Repetition is the daily bread which satisfies with benediction . . . . Life is a repetition."[10] Despite this philosopher's sanguine viewpoint, repetition has serious negative aspects. Through repeated depictions in television programs and press releases, does violence become modern man's daily bread, reinforcing an attitude of callousness toward death and destruction? The quotation in a cartoon depicting a television announcer is apropos: "The following program will provide you with 100 per cent of your daily minimum requirement of violence, bloodshed and mayhem."[11]

The constant repetition in the mass media may have created an attitude on the part of observers that says: "I don't give a damn; it doesn't concern me; I'm removed; I don't want to get involved." Similarly, unrelieved confrontation with threatening news can lead to an anxiety that is ironically expressed as "there's nothing I can do about it, so why bother?"[12] Although in and of itself, repetition does not inspire or motivate, it has an undeniably significant effect on behavior. According to an old adage, repetition is the mother of learning. It is just as useful to call it the mother of unlearning, for the consequences of indifference and similar attitudes demobilize and debilitate what should otherwise be a healthy society.

In the mass media, the drops of communication that fall unceasingly upon plastic minds must obviously result in what psychologist William James called "walking bundles of habits."[13] The constant dripping of water will bore a hole in the hardest stone.

Another phenomenon called apperception occurs when an idea, fact, or attitude is assimilated with and linked to other ideas already in the mind. When repetition and apperception work together, learning undeniably results. In advertising, propaganda, and entertainment, repetition and apperception are highly effective ways of teaching the value of anything from energy conservation and war bonds, hair spray and cola drinks to liquor and tobacco, love and hate.

Promotions, slogans, household information, products and personalities are learned unconsciously from newspapers, magazines, television, and recordings. Unwittingly, an individual imitates the actions presented and soon finds himself with a habit. While people absorb the content from an unbalanced news report or a one-sided drama, the interrupting advertisement may send them to the kitchen for a can of beer or make them reach for a cigarette.

When a young person views a film or enjoys a magazine or a paper-back book in which dozens of bullets are used to kill a victim, he or she may not be moved by confrontation with reports of actual violence. Listening ten thousand times a season to the discs of a performing ensemble at an ear-dinning audio level is apt to leave little alternative but to assimilate. When, in some cases, anti-social behavior results, this is, in part, because the media have represented the violent, the absurd and the caco-phonic as an accepted, major part of social institutions.

Imagine the consequences if all citizens heard and read and repeated to themselves the Golden Rule as often as they heard and repeated that a certain brand "tastes good like a cigarette should" or that they are "a Pepsi generation" and "things go better with Coke." Consider that an in-structor who queries a typical high school or college class may find the Golden Rule to be almost unheard of among students, let alone medi-tated, verbalized, or repeated. Many illustrations of the prevalence of imi-tation in daily life can be made to show that teachers and members of the media need to share a passionate enthusiasm for values in their own in-tellectual lives, especially the value that genuine respect for the well-being of others is rewarded by society. Then the learning flame is constructively ignited.

In brief, teachers, as well as parents, must understand that attitudes and behaviors are not always taught by direct instruction. They are learned almost without awareness by an exposure to examples inviting imitation. In the classroom or in the mass media imitation and repetition are suggested and inspired; they are not necessarily part of conscious teaching. The response is one of more or less unthinking adoption rather than of thoughtful judgment. No educator need, therefore, blandly dis-trust the media, but he ought rather to help them communicate worthy examples.

MOTIVATION

Some critics of the schools bemoan a decadent modern youth with little motivation to study. The fact is, however, that youth have not basi-cally changed in their attitude toward genuine learning any more than the demands of learning have changed. Youth of previous generations de-tested books and book learning as much as do today's youngsters. College and university students have traditionally been suspected of an inherent inclination to shun or slide over serious study, to crave the excitement of pranks and sundry extracurricular activities.

In his book, *College or Kindergarten?*, Max McConn lists three pur-poses that motivate college attendance: (1) The Bread-and-Butter Pur-pose . . . to afford special privilege and a differential advantage in the economic struggle to those few, including themselves, who may be shrewd and thrifty and enterprising enough to seize the opportunity presented; (2) The Superkindergarten Purpose . . . to take care of a group of older babíes, who have progressed, in their amusements, from rattles to rah-rahs! . . . (3) The Culture Purpose . . . the transmission of culture— of knowledge and beauty and understanding and of a delight in these things and in their uses in the world.[14]

The Bread-and-Butter Purpose is vocational. The Superkindergarten Purpose embraces the range of extracurricular activities on campus: parties, dances, lectures, elections and all student projects and meetings not required as course assignments. The only genuinely educational motivation lies in the Culture Purpose, which many students and some faculty members rank at the bottom of the list.

An educator cannot assume that the mind needs, desires and welcomes culture for its intellectual value, and that a thirst for knowledge can be relied upon. There is little basis for this view in daily experience or in the observation of formal schooling. Centuries ago, Aristotle in his book of *Politics*, wrote that learning is no teen-age amusement, like mere music satisfying youth without pain.[15] Due to the influence of mass media, the simplest, the most comfortable, the most appealing or satisfying method of presentation is now expected by youth even in the classroom. Serious, intensive and prolonged study has always been a matter of unnatural effort for most human beings and is even more so today.

If a person is invited to an academic lecture or a movie with an acknowledged message, he or she is apt immediately to avoid it. Something in most people resists predesignated learning. Jay Haley, writing in *Quarterly of Film, Radio, and Television*, has stated, "A housewife faced with the possibility of war, with an irritating husband, or with rising prices does not head for a campus lecture on international relations, psychology, or economics. She says, 'I have to go to a movie tonight, or I'll be batty!' "[16]

More immediate and glittering than classes are the rewards of wide open spaces, daring pursuits, exciting contests or sensational love. More pleasant than the drone and drudgery of books and classes is the lulling aura of rest or sleep. Joseph Hart, an authority on the social interpretation of education, virtually indicts the schools with this comment: "Few people who have safely escaped from school care anything for more knowledge. Teachers care for it only as it furthers their chances in life. The average adult demands knowledge when it has meaning for his personal experience and even then he gets on very well without it . . . . We are not fundamentally knowing beings."[17]

Partly in recognition of these hard facts, a formal system of public instruction has traditionally used a variety of enforcement measures. To encourage and insure school attendance, the social expectations of family, friends, and community have operated as a powerful factor. Equally manifest are the forces of government, of industry and business, the goal of a job and its salary, and administrative and curricular requirements in education. Yet the motivation is still lacking in many cases.

When the pressures to be educated are absorbed by an individual, they in themselves can become motivations in varying degrees. These motivations have changed little on high school and college campuses over recent years; they are bound up in words such as "career," "success," "making money," "social climbing," and "athletics." They give opportunity to persons to overcome handicaps of birth, poverty, or character. Educational pursuit becomes motivated largely "as a tool of social ambition," and "the most effective means of social advancement."[18]

The role of motivation in the mass media is widespread. As related to socio-economic status, sex, intelligence and other factors, certain forces in people have for generations intrigued philosophers, sociologists, psychologists and other theorizers. Successively called "instincts," "drives," and "motives," they have been elaborately listed, defined, disagreed upon, refined and extended. Hundreds of research and study reports continue to be published each year. There can be little disagreement, however, that among people's basic motivations are those enumerated by sociologist William J. Thomas, namely *security, response, recognition* and *new experience*.[19] Operators of the mass media, one may be sure, fully utilize these motivations in planning content and appeal.

Everyone seeks *security* to provide for bodily necessities and to acquire property as protection against illness and old age. Some call it the instinct for self-preservation. A universal interest in security may be noted in news items relating to national affairs and foreign policy, cost of living and unemployment, developments in science, stock market trends, and weather reports. It helps to enlarge the flood of "do-it-yourself" books, articles, and programs in the almost every conceivable area of living.

The need for *response*, for giving and receiving affection, for feeling that someone wants the love an individual can offer, is basic in all human beings. The huge success of such paperbacks as *How to Win Friends and Influence People* is a prominent example. Frequently the search for response is satisfied only vicariously—the substitute forms of social contact offered by radio and television drama fill the gap for many. Similarly, one may find in the popular lovelorn columns and in the romantic movies and fiction responses that are engendered through identification and empathy.

A young person distraught over self-identity finds reassurance through insight into human motivations portrayed on the media. They offer a reaffirmation of status, the comforting recognition that no matter what his or her life is like, someone else is undergoing similar experiences and problems, and something will happen to make all come out well in the end.

Motivated by the desire for *recognition*, men and women strive for prestige and respect from a social group. They want to be among the first to be "in the know," to have read the latest books, seen the new movie, played the "hit" recording, and heard or read the "scoop" in the stripteaser's court trial. They desire to impress others by erudite-sounding conversation on media content. From childhood on, reading brings rewards from parents and teachers; later, the pleasant associations with reading continue in such approved symbols as "good literature," "fine books" and the "classics." "Doing the right thing" motivates listening to religious broadcasts on Sunday morning, attending a film on social problems, or reading a book on human relations.

Men and women yearn to change their routine of activity and environment, to have *new experiences*. They seek respite, escape, and adventure in far-off places. Writers on the subject of popular culture suggest that when people feel deprived and alienated, they turn to a dreamlike world for substitute gratification.[20] When an imprisoned emotion is tapped, writes Erik Barnouw in his book *Mass Communication*, ". . . we sense in the secret charade of identification, a chance to circumvent taboos we dare not violate, win old battles already lost, lock firmly trap doors still quivering beneath us."[21]

A sense of relaxation that evades the frustrations, anxieties and boredom of the daily grind comes conveniently to millions when they join the great audiences attending the movies, listening to the radio, looking at television, reading comic strips or novels, or playing stereo records. For millions of young people, the escapism of the media largely satisfies their characteristic yearning for romance, their insatiable appetite for wonder and admiration.

One may regard motivation as primary, in the sense of native physical requirements for food, drink, rest and protection; or secondary in the sense of its being social and cultural. Psychologist Abraham Maslow has attempted to show how drives alter and mature into purposes by listing them in a kind of hierarchical order beginning with those appearing first in life. This is his list: gratification of bodily needs, safety insurance against pain and danger of life, love, affection, warmth, acceptance, self-esteem, self-respect, self-confidence, feelings of strength and adequacy; self-actualization, self-fulfillment, self-expression, full use of one's capacities.[22]

Beyond these motivations, there is for most people an unmistakable appeal in any activity that possesses liveliness. Like new experience, this embraces the excitement of sports events, action drama, and sensational reporting. It is behind the statements of youth who say, "Classes are too slow, too dead; we need something live like television." Says one creative student: "Few teachers are alive, hep to the real world . . . . What a profession! It's composed of squares and dullards."[23]

The implication is not that mathematics, history or Shakespeare are dull; rather it is that the techniques employed to capture interest and to win attention are ineffective, especially as they relate to the subjects of basic needs and drives of youth and adults and to the day-to-day influences of the mass media. The fault lies in the incapacity, hesitation, or unwillingness of teachers to rouse vital motivations, their failure to excite a student through the use of the vivid techniques of the mass media.

Mass communication succeeds in teaching largely because it opens, as a key does a lock, the emotionally repressed areas of millions, in much the same way as does fantasy for a child. The central truth is that attention flows from interest, that learning has personal value. In their study of the teaching-learning process, Nathaniel Cantor and Stephen Corey stated: "Compelled conformity is not goodness but the response to fear and anxiety . . . . It is surrendering to the will of power and authority. It breeds submissiveness, hostility, and resentment, and it frequently leads to a denial of those feelings and to self-justification for the shoddy performance. This actually robs the pupil of self-responsibility and self-discipline."[24]

Perhaps it is largely a motivation connection with recognition and new experience and a contagion of suggested models to imitate, plus the prime time and space which the media give to sensational events that explains much of the notoriety in our society. This media implication is the subject of a report by David Gelman on the criticism of the mass media for their coverage of the twin assassination attempts against President Ford in September 1975.[25] "Lurid headlines, vivid details about the lives of the two would-be assassins and football-style instant replay on television" recall the Watergate trauma, the series of kidnappings following the Patty Hearst venture and the Los Angeles' Watts riots, and dramatize the question of whether the media directly contribute to an atmosphere that fosters violence. Both *Time* and *Newsweek* were accused of conferring cover-girl status on Squeaky Fromme. A more serious question for educators is whether the public schools did not also lend assistance by inadvertently teaching young people to yearn for and seek sensational and repeated publicity at any cost to self and society.

The ultimate responsibility for motivation rests with the learner. All genuine education is, in the last analysis, obtained through self-learning and self-discipline. Compulsory class attendance, the threat of bad grades and failure, the promise of reward, parental or school pressure toward competitive striving will not lead to true and productive learning unless the student is truly motivated. His learning discipline lies in overcoming difficulties and making discoveries on his own. He really teaches himself. The professional teacher can only make available the sources and the environment for learning.

LEARNING FROM THE MASS MEDIA

Fortunately, schools operate largely on the principle that selected learning is an attractive goal for everyone. It is assumed or believed on faith that every learner has some desire to be actively motivated and goal-seeking, not only in routine living but also in intelligent and progressive learning. From all of society and nature, through a variety of media, the learner inevitably perceives, accepts, sifts, and develops manifold stimuli in accordance with his own predispositions toward self-development. The concept of the human vegetable, apparently and unfortunately utilized by some individuals in teaching and communication, is disastrous.

Formal schooling is a structured presentation of experience, activities, and content that will permit the learner to acquire the behavior of an educated person. A knowing mind must be locked in union with a seeking mind. The classroom does not succeed if it only provides the kind of stimulus pattern that enables a learner to know answers in the classroom, while inhibiting his knowing them in the real-life situation. Similarly, it fails if it relies solely on the giving of tests in order to determine whether learning has taken place. Quite obviously, there may be classroom learning and zero retention; one may pursue a citizenship course in high school or college and later ignore the polls and the democratic process.

Conversely, one may attend thoughtfully to radio and television viewpoints on campaign issues. One may have heard of the Teapot Dome Scandal in social studies and later have transferred this knowledge to the events known as the Watergate Scandal.

"The main effect of communication," wrote Wilbur Schramm, "is on the pictures in our heads, our cognitive maps of environment, our images of ourselves, the beliefs and values we have accepted and are prepared to defend, the evaluations we have made of our relationships to individuals and groups."[26] The mass media sharpen the fact that learning can happen any time.

Classroom learning will wither if teachers remain blind to the capabilities of the mass media. Guided by a principle of "one skill under one skull," their students concentrate on sharpening a finely-selected, slenderly-tapering spear of knowledge to a finer and finer point. This is unfortunately a grinding process meant to result in immediate and tangible success. The broader, liberal approach to learning has been shifted to a "background drama" remote from the classroom. For the rest of his life, a student educated in this way will be capable only of passive learning, chiefly via commercially prompted television, recordings, movies and publishing.

Of course, it should be made clear that the mass media vary in the extent to which they are passive presences in a person's life or inciters to positive learning and behavior. The programs on television offer a very limited choice at any one moment. While the books in a library can be almost limitless in number and variety, an individual more often than not must have a fairly definite notion of what he wants to read if he is really to benefit. A person's reading requires a more complicated act of choice than in the case of radio or television; it must be considerably self-propelled.

The significant relationship of the mass media to learning is this: the process of learning and the principles of motivation and self-development are operative in a continuing process, in a more intimate and less vicarious part of total living than a classroom provides. Teachers and teaching, educators assert, make up a channel through which the culture of society is transmitted. Teaching, they say, involves the continuous encouraging of students to act, the stimulating of a pupil toward correct thinking and behavior, and the making of impressions on the mind and heart that are to last forever.

The educator must himself adopt and develop these truths and recognize the usefulness of the modern mass media in the learning process. The mass media have the potential to offer intellectual enjoyment and stimulating challenge. They can lead to curiosity about people, places and events, and to improved knowledge, discussion, thinking, and reading. In brief, the mass media confront one squarely with the fact that teaching and learning are an inseparable partnership in education, both formal and informal.

6

HARNESSING THE POWER OF THE MASS MEDIA

Who communicates what to whom, by what means, in what convenient setting of place and time, for what purpose, with what effect? In this question, adapted from an analysis by Harold Lasswell at Columbia University,[1] lies an apt formula for describing the process of modern public communications. Here the communicator (the who), the content (the what), the media (the means), the audience (the whom), the setting (the where and when), and the purpose or goal all converge on an ultimate objective: impact. One writes, speaks, or performs for the mass media for one primary reason: to produce mass effect. The process is one of the total culture, its creation and its distribution; the prime mover in the sequence is the communicator.

The communicator is the performing artist on television, radio, or in recordings. This person is the program manager, actor, comedian, acrobat, or commentator. He or she is the writer, editor, columnist, or layout person. He or she may be a featured individual or may share a role with others. Numerous supporting roles are filled at the transmitting end of the communications process. Mass communicators plan and edit newspapers, magazines, books, films and broadcasts; organize the news gatherers into press associations; and advertise products and services. They report the achievements and shortcomings of people in public office; shine a public spotlight on the activities of antisocial groups and individuals; interpret the interests of all people, including minorities, in a better way of life; and persuade a community and government to act. They entertain in many ways to suit the tastes and moods of varied audiences.

The effect of a public communication depends on each of the elements of the communications process; it depends on the subject or script. Nothing is lost or gained if one chooses either to simplify or to mystify the elements by espousing Marshall McLuhan's dictum, "The medium is the massage." Yet, the effect of the media is much more complex; it depends on which medium is used, for each has its own peculiar qualities of transmission and atmosphere. According to Joseph Klapper, author of *The Effects of Mass Communications*, the communicating carries "among and through a nexus of mediating factors and influences."[2]

Without question, the effect of communication depends also on those whose eyes and ears it reaches in the audiences. Very young minds dwell on the comics in a newspaper; they attend to the cartoons and commercials on television. In books they look at the pages with color and pictures. During their first ten years, youngsters fall under a strong influence of family patterns; during the next ten, reading skills, broader knowledge, peer groups, and teen-age uncertainties are major influences. Older minds, on the other hand, turn to the printed pages of news and sports, programs of drama and music, and recordings and books of prose and poetry. In movies, the preferences vary with age groups, from slapstick, adventure, mystery-horror, history-biography, and serious drama.

Once the content of a communication reaches a certain audience via a particular medium or combination of media, the environment of the recipient, his mood, his health, his personal associations, and countless variables and relationships enter into any effect the media have. For the practical purpose of a mass medium, the effect is intimately related to the size of the audience. This size, actual and potential, drives and motivates the communicator.

THE COMMUNICATOR AND EFFECT

Some speakers, performers, artists, or writers may feel that they speak or perform or write or create as they please, but the moment a person wishes to communicate regularly via the mass media, he largely subordinates his own pleasure to that of the audience, to his sponsor, and to the media entrepreneurs who hold audience size and response to be of primary importance.

It is this value placed on audience effect that impels the communicator to move forward. Almost ruthlessly he operates on the principle that any communications effort must have a recognizable effect or it is in vain. From the moment he takes his product—its content and his talents—to the mass media, he knows that it enters a highly competitive marketplace. There are the vast audiences to reach, numerous behaviors to change, and ideas to forge among millions of people.

COMPARISON AND CONTRAST BETWEEN PUBLIC EDUCATION AND PUBLIC COMMUNICATION		
The Elements of the Formula	*Public Education (Schools and Colleges) (Noncommercial)*	*Public Communication (Mass Media) (Largely commercial)*
Who	*Teachers (assisted by school staff and administration)*	Communicators—commentators, entertainers, musicians, actors writers, editors, advertisers, etc. (assisted by staff and crew)
What	*Curriculum (courses and subject matter which educate but which also inform, enlighten, inspire, and entertain)*	Content that is information, enlightenment, and inspiration, along with education
To whom	*Pupils or students in age and grade groups averaging up to thirty*	Mass audiences of a million or more, including pupils or students
By what means	*Demonstration, discussion, textbook assignments, audiovisual aids, libraries, etc.*	Mass media of radio, recordings, television and movies; and the press media of newspapers, magazines, and mass market paperbacks
In what setting	*Classroom, largely formal*	Everywhere, mainly the home, largely informal, with movies largely also in theaters
When	*9 A.M. to 4 P.M., Monday through Friday, nine months of the year, exclusive of weekends and holidays, during years of childhood and youth*	Constantly and repeatedly twenty-four hours a day all year round, for a lifetime; with some conditions of dissemination, such as movie theater schedules, or availability of a record player or radio
Why, or for what purpose	*To develop sound minds in healthy bodies for happy lives and better citizens*	To provide the kinds of services for sufficiently large audiences as will bring monetary gain
Effects	*Changing people's lives*	Changing people's lives.

The communicator cares about that audience and its response to his word and gesture. He cares so much that, on the basis of his personality and talents, he selects only the content that will actually convey his message to the world and its audiences. He often has a certain segment of the population in mind. His content may be for lovers, for parents, for sports fans, or for headache sufferers. The subjects of love, parenthood, headaches, food, recreation or humor are not at every moment of universal interest, but the communicator never hides the fact that he is always hoping the whole world is hearing or reading or viewing his message with appreciation. The public communicator presumes that his message is for everyone, and he adores the whole world for attending to him. He expects it to.

His ultimate effect may be one of entertainment, of information, or of persuasion for people to act a certain way or purchase a certain product. Moreover, the goal with which he is constantly concerned is building his audience size into more and more millions. Then, he believes, the ultimate effects will follow. His product will be sold, his performance will entertain or inform or inspire and his message will become part of the culture.

When the audience is large enough and the effect of a message is strong and positive enough, a reverse flow is assured, and the communications process is fully successful. The concept of feedback takes on meaning. The audience stimulates the communicator much as the roar of the crowd sustains the actor. He works even harder in the knowledge that his contribution is acceptable and desired on the widest possible scale. He is inspired by the audience, and he asks, as his greatest reward, for a chance to communicate to them again and again.

The professional-minded mass communicator is not a mere rubber stamp for the desires and demands of the masses. He is a man of honest conviction. As did George Washington, he can ask, "If to please the people, we offer what we ourselves disapprove, how can we afterward defend our work?"[4] The professional communicator is aware of what the members of an audience need and ought to have. He is not without originality and creativity and, most of all, not without standards. He knows that these must be blended with what the audience wants or can be successfully encouraged to accept. He makes every effort to ensure that his offerings will be the happy balance between actual needs and expressed desires.

The communicator develops the realistic view of an executive whose time is largely spent in moving ideas and information from his mind to other minds. "Nothing happens in business—or in the professions or in government—until somebody communicates," states a handbook on dictating correspondence.[5] Anyone who works with his mind rather than his hands depends for his influence and his success on how effectively he gets across what he knows, thinks and feels. At his command are not only manuals, but also scholarly treatises, outlining and describing methods of captivating large audiences. From these and their own experiences, the director trained in public relations, the producer versed in the arts of the theater, and the publisher skilled in promotion and distribution of books may be the teachers of many speakers, writers, artists or performers. These front-line communicators, in turn, are masters of the skills themselves.

In a sense, the techniques involve the traditional forms of persuasion "writ large." Among these are such psychological concepts as suggestion, conduciveness, rationalization, repetition, word manipulation, "the big lie," and these appeal to the human needs for togetherness, common grounds, prestige and a scapegoat.[6] Much of the analysis of audience motivation and appeal can be stated as principles of mass persuasion.[7] The message must reach the sense organs of the persons who are to be influenced. Thus, the media can stimulate only those who perceive it. Also, the prevailing cognitive structure of any mind tends to resist, distort, or reject stimulus to change. New ideas must have some relationship to the old.

Any action of the recipient, any positive response to media stimuli, must be seen as a path toward some goal. The more a specific path of action is located at a time or in a situation requiring a decision or step of action, the more likely it is that the action will take place.

Viewed another way, the techniques of mass communication include the common devices of propaganda, as they are aptly summarized by the Institute for Propaganda Analysis, an organization that operated as a service to citizens just prior to World War II. They are (a) the glittering generality, or the association of an idea with a virtue word; (b) the transfer of sanction or prestige to whatever one is promoting in order to make it respectable; (c) the testimonial from some respected person that a given idea or program or product is good; (d) the "plain folks" technique used by a speaker to convince an audience that he and his ideas are trustworthy because they are of the people; (e) card stacking, or the arranging of facts or falsehoods, illustrations or distractions, in order to present the best (or the worst) possible case for an idea, program, person or product; and (f) the band wagon theme that "everybody is doing it."[8]

Other techniques take the form of sensationalism. The stress may be on the fantastic or stupendous as in Hollywood extravaganzas, or the shocking, as in a magazine cover on sex, or on the splash of the grotesque, as in radio mystery drama. Audiences are largely thought of as creatures who taste, smell, see, hear, and feel before they are creatures who reason or who think of others. Historians of the mass media who are inclined toward over-generalizations may recall the twentieth century as the

Age of Sensationalism. They may contrast it with the Age of Rationalism or Age of Humanism.

The cultivation of a feeling of participation is also important for developing "a sense of potential energy in the receiving audience which is translatable into the kinetic."[9] From a sense of social role and obligation, people will buy a product, join a crusade, go to the polls, visit a library— in brief, they will be stimulated to act. Persuasion brings results more quickly by involving people in an activity, rather than by merely preaching or teaching about it. This lesson may also be applied to the classroom. Communication requires the use of persuasive techniques but without the propaganda, the overt appeal to the senses and feelings, and the abuse of sensationalism.

Vulgarity, Violence and Other Evils

The techniques of persuasion and public relations are all directed toward the end of maximum audience effect. Unhappily, the limitless power of these techniques through the media of mass communications may parallel a limitless dependence on mediocrity, irrationality and emotionalism. So apparent is this dependence that a variety and quantity of criticisms as endless as they are unbelievable have been leveled at the media.

The communications process, critics have been saying for two decades, is pockmarked with qualities of the second-rate and with the preferences of the twelve-year-old intelligence. "Since Mass Culture is not an art form but a manufactured commodity," according to one gloomy theory, "it tends always downward, toward cheapness—and so toward standardization of production."[10] Coining a word for newspapers, radio, magazines and television altogether, one critic wrote: "Masscom's delight in the shoddy, the tasteless, the mind-dulling, the useless is well established."[11] An article entitled "Where is television going?" declares: "No civilization in history has so openly published to itself and to the world its cultural mediocrity, its moral shallowness, the emptiness of its alienated spirit, and the paucity of public conscience, despite its superlative excellence in technological and scientific endeavor."[12]

Among the endless, unbelievable criticisms leveled at the media are the following: The printed page is filled with "drivel, sex and scapel." The magazines are all the same, containing "bosoms and butts, high heels, opera hose, leopard skins, manacles, whips and wrestling ladies."[13] Best-seller blurbs show obscenity on the bookstands in the form of such quotations as "sewer-written by authors for dirty-minded readers."[14] Other charges leveled against the media include the fact that pornographic magazines and paperbacks dwell "on every conceivable profane and gutter term to describe in minute and lurid detail any form of hetero- and homosexual aberration."[15] The flood of pornography is now torrential, and the gates are wide open to almost everyone. The covers and pages of "girlie," male-oriented and detective magazines are said to incite youth and adults to release normal inhibitions. They have "no purpose except pictorial prostitution."[16] The horrors of comic books make readers "unconsciously delighted" at seeing women beaten up and shot; they "seem to enlarge upon the most perverse aspects of the human conscience."[17] Comic book horrors are the "prep school for the totalitarian society."[18]

Movies for two generations have featured the "kissin' and the shootin'." Criminal daring on the screen arouses a desire for easy money and luxury; crime techniques suggest methods for achieving them. The themes of lawlessness and aberration prevail. Brazen displays of lovemaking stir the passions toward socially unacceptable outlets.[19] The highly publicized attractions of the 1960s were reproached for being about brothels, incest, lesbian teachers, a crazy rapist, or a nymphomaniac.[20] By the early 1970s pornographic movie houses had sprung up in most cities and box office lines reached peak lengths for nationally promoted films called "skin flicks." Every sexual fantasy was laid bare—"girls copulating with horses and pigs, views of sexually connected couples . . . gyrating to music, and the zoom lens of the camera probing every pore, recess and hair in the pink and white tissue of male and female genitalia."[21]

The attacks on radio have been relentless during its many decades of existence. "Radio is as brash as a peanut vendor in a lecture hall, it's as cheap as a popcorn hawker at the opera, it's a burp in an anthem."[22] Soon after its beginning, its terrible deed became the annihilation of silence. Now, states one observer, it has become almost entirely "back-talk and noise." In its new life, it is "a hard-nosed, brassy, money-grubbing harlot . . . background to the other clatter in America, polluter of the air, adding a steady rhythm of din and commercial carnivalia to the land."[23] Perhaps the most basic issue yet to be decided is "whether radio is to be clown or man."[24]

As the most recent and pervasive mass medium, television bears the brunt of the most prevalent satire and cynicism and the most alarming fears. Television presents mostly "blood, sex and steers." It is "a triumph of equipment over people," a form of entertainment that has doomed the next generation to becoming "wide-bottomed, one-eyed morons,"[25] with "eyeballs as big as cantaloupes and no brain at all."[26] Television has been called an "idiot box," a "boob tube," and "hellish boredom," the flow of "two hundred millions of absolutely free monads, billions of free words and pictures going straight into the hell of emptiness."[27] It is "a vast wasteland, an endless succession of electronic comic books."[28] It may prove as "dangerous to culture as the atom bomb is to civilization." A university chancellor reads the future: "Under the impact of television I can contemplate a time in America when people can neither read nor write, but will be no better than the forms of plant life."[29]

Television inundates our lives "with death and disaster one moment, trivia and banality the next," a *Look* magazine article reported.[30] In the view of an anonymous critic, the audience is led to think more and more "with its testes and ovaries." According to the final report of the National Commission on the Causes and Prevention of Violence, television portrays a world in which good guys and bad guys alike use violence as a legitimate means for solving problems and attaining desired goals.[31] In a similar vein, an observer analyzes the audience: "Video-addicts keep expecting an easy solution. When it doesn't come, they grow impatient, then adamant or disillusioned. Soon they believe *they* are defective. Instead of coming of age, they're coming apart."[32] They comprise "a nation of videots."

Those who attack the mass media for these and any other evils are concerned largely with the effects of repetitious presentation. According to one among many such reports, the average child in the United States by the age of 14 has spent 22,000 hours in front of a television set, has been bombarded by about 350,000 commercials and witnessed the assault on or destruction of more than 18,000 people.[33] In millions of identical copies, issues, or releases, day after day, hour after hour, depending upon the medium, the same or a similar message assaults the recipients—Mr. and Mrs. Public and Family—and reinforces responses they have already made. The content leads nowhere and gives nothing to reach for. At best, it is non-education; at worst, it is anti-education.

How constant the repetition of a message can be without becoming intolerable varies with the individual critic and his particular standards. Most people dislike persistent callousness or catering to weakness of character. If, for example, one opposes only gross indulgence in violence, liquor and tobacco, none of these vices in isolation may be a moral issue. The moderate person is uncomfortable, however, with the thought that the unharnessed force of mass media content may push us all into a brutish, drunken, puffing, sex-bent conformity. In the receptive mind, the repeated experience of advertising or of programs that play up human vices creates a world in which thoughts and acts of violence, unnecessary vices and undesirable habits appear to be normal and to set the standards.

As far back as 1941, the authors of a report for the American Council on Education held that the constant repetition of the unrealities of the movies has unavoidable influence on youth and other persons.[34] The real danger is not that they will lead a young person into immorality or crime but that they may distort his picture of human existence." Naive conceptions of romance, stereotyped language and stock patterns of human relationships exaggerate trivialities and diminish ideals of excellence for people. A stock motive is to show revenge as "natural, necessary and heroic."[35] A stock theme is the inability of human beings to liberate themselves from the nuclear sword hanging over their heads. One may ask whether the mass media do not prolong an ominous quiet about kill and overkill, as described in Ralph Lapp's book on the strategy of annihilation, where he wrote that "the human race looks like sheep marching silently to slaughter."[36]

Brutality appears as a widespread behavior and a permissible reality; it is tolerated with little or no criticism; it is frequently imitated. Murder, violence and crime are attention-getters intended to hold the millions so that they will also submit to the advertising. One authority has even dubbed those movies and programs and headlines dwelling on war as "war commercials."[37] Frances Hennock, former chairman of the Federal Communications Commission, said that this kind of programming "cannot help but convey to the minds of the immature viewers the impression that crime, violence, brutality and horror are the most conspicuous features of life."[38] Presented merely for the repeated amusement of the spectator and the profit of the sponsor, murder is no longer a classic experience in tragedy that touches the innermost being of man, as the existentialist philosopher Karl Jaspers asserts.[39] Rather, it is a salable media commodity around which has developed a household vocabulary about torture and executions. Despite some findings to the contrary, the enactment of murder in the mass media is a motivating force for the person on the verge of hate or revenge, a vision in the mind of the amused spectator for recall at some later moment. No one has yet proved that this was not the case in the minds of a presidential killer and his murderer or in the minds of other assassins.

Commercially contrived bad taste in art is called "kitsch," a term that can readily be applied to the media. Oversold and inescapable, the kitsch of the media forces upon millions a gross perversion of violence and sex. By no means is it a problem of the subject matter itself, for the *Bible* presents violence and sex frequently; dramatic works such as *Hamlet* portray incest, insanity, infidelity and poisoning; and other masterpieces of literature, music and other arts nakedly portray the depths of human passion and cruelty. Writing on freedom and communications, Dan Lacy describes the mass media perversion as a disassociation of sex and violence from the human realities that give them meaning, using them as gimmicks to spice up an advertisement or catch attention at the newsstand.[40] Sex and violence are part of the fabric of life and to ban them would be to ban the best of literature, including the *Bible*. The problem, then, is not one of censorship, but of temperance and judgment, lest the themes gain an inordinate attention and a glorification that eventually tear human existence to shreds.

Less excitable and engaging to observe than murder, but extensively repeated throughout the mass media, is the acting out of drunkenness. When it is made the subject of comedy, as it so often is, it has little chance of being recognized as the disease of alcoholism. Suspecting that very explicit advertising in England has been proceeding on the premise that "people buy booze to get bombed," the Advertising Standards Authority asks for limits on proclaiming the attributes of alcoholic beverages.[41]

Columnist Marilynn Preston writes: "Talk about your media overkill, I'd have to call our session media overspill since, for three solid hours, we were blitzed and shpritzed repeatedly with incident after incident involving liquor." She quotes William Hathaway, head of the Senate Subcommittee on Narcotics and Alcohol: "Many millions of American youth are bombarded every day with many thousands of messages about drinking from many hundreds of glamorous, friendly, healthy, adventurous, sexy—and in some cases, venomous—people telling them of the joys and benefits of drinking." It is made to appear normal for everyone, at home no less than in a bar.[42]

Mass media repetition is also a chief reason for the long-standing, undisputed position of cigarettes as a necessity for millions in our society. The tobacco industry opposition to any public efforts to discourage smoking has been strong. A proposed air-pollution tax on smokers is of mixed benefit, for it is also a way of making cigarette sales important to the public treasury. It was only with much reluctance that cigarette manufacturers opted for restraint in their mass advertising among the youth market.

For decades a nondrinker or a nonsmoker had become someone not quite healthy, hearty or sportsmanlike. Having reached the early teens, a cautious boy, in particular, often endured such labels as "sissy" or "chicken." The practice continues of regarding only those with a liquor glass or beer can in hand as possessing virility or as qualified to associate with "men of distinction." Only the young lady with a cigarette between her lips is entitled to the accolade, "You've come a long way, baby!" Stress on moderation or on abstinence rarely appears without some kind of apology, since, for so long, it ran counter to established commercial interests and social images.

Massacre on the highways may result in an occasional public warning that drinking and driving do not mix. Cancer research and Federal Trade Commission findings may scare a smoker now and then and antismoking commercials may appear hourly, but those who campaign against either of these vices are likely to find this a largely hopeless task, for the mass media use of the techniques of persuasion have had overwhelming success. Some observers believe that despite scientific reports from trusted government sources in England and the United States (and despite the facts presented in college courses in physiology, health and physical recreation) Jane and John Q. Public would rather die than take a firm stand on tobacco and liquor independent of mass media persuasion.

Commercial sponsors with a message may swarm to television as an advertising medium because it commands strong sustained attention, but they do not neglect the importance of continuing to bring this same message via all the media. Research findings do not support a popular assumption that the media compete among each other for audiences. Audience overlap is extensive: Moviegoers are also radio listeners, magazine readers are also television fans, and nearly all of these read one or more newspapers and buy recordings and paperback books. As a *Business Week* magazine article enjoins its readers, business people can softly embrace all channels to urge a mass public to purchase their product.[43] Multimedia advertising firms quickly rise to give aid and to help assure better results.

John Keats, in his book, *The Crack in the Picture Window*, makes several indictments of the media: Dwellers in housing developments, he notes, oppressed by ennui, turn to the mass communications media to find new ideas. But because "everyone sees the same TV shows, reads the same article in the same magazine, they all come up with the same ideas at the same time, and the result is more ennui." The humdrum is reinforced and the variation in taste further lessened, he writes, when the mediamen angle their productions for the housing development public.[44]

"Mass media isolate one morally from other men, from life and from one's self, and the bored and lonely feeling continues," psychoanalyst Ernest Van den Haag declared on a lecture tour when he was at the New School for Social Research.[45] The mass media repetition and oversimplified approach even to accepted works such as plays, paintings, and sculpture destroy their enriching qualities. In this view, everything that is beautiful can be destroyed by overuse. Art, music and poetry become meaningless clichés when continually exposed to people who do not try to understand them. Repetition and overuse lead to orgy. The daily and hourly displays of passion and caprices, whims and fancies roll out without ceasing, stripping away the veneer of civilization. Despite the interpretations of supreme courts, a magazine editorial insists that the Constitution does not encourage the media repeatedly to cross the line from reporting events to exploiting them for commercial purposes.[46]

INEFFECTIVENESS OF CRITICISM

The outcries of professional and lay individuals and groups are loud enough to incite periodic investigations of the methods and content of the mass media. On a national scale, legislative committees, the Federal Communications Commission and the Department of Justice have become actively involved. The attacks seem endless and everywhere, and one wonders how the media have continued to operate and enjoy any reputation. Yet, the enthusiasm and freedom of the communicator and the sensationalism and repetition of the content seem to continue unabated as much after the criticisms as before. Why have government action, professional criticism, and citizen disgust been relatively ineffective?

One might observe that much of the content of the mass media represents vested economic interests. A critic's plea that the mass media urge moderation or abstinence in the use of a highly advertised product could lead to the decline of livelihood for countless employees and their managers in particular industries. Critics leave well enough alone in this area. The normal response of persons who would be affected would be indifference or resistance. The latter could take the form of lobbying and other interest group tactics that counteract the criticism and leave the mass media revolution unabated.

Criticism lacks validity if authoritative research does not support it. Therefore, the assertions that some media offerings cause delinquency or crime are seen only as personal opinion. They may be made without knowledge or consciousness of any fair standards of good or bad, of right or wrong. When stemming from government, the efforts to restrain or improve communications are often regarded as meddling and even destructive. When they have come from educators and have not been accompanied by constructive alternatives, they have been merely numbing and have been accounted envious or niggling.

Because the effect is the result of several forces, the influences of violence and other kinds of immorality on the mass media viewing public have not been well established. The communicator can shape his message and decide when and where to communicate it, and his is a primary role. But any response also depends upon the situation in which the communication is received, the personality of the receiver, and his group relationships and standards. A simple, causal relationship between the content of the communication and its effect in any kind of "one way" or "transmission belt" fashion cannot be assumed.

After all, countless facts of Biblical and other ancient historical times establish that adultery, greed, and bloodshed occurred and reoccurred long before comic books, *Playboy* and *Gunsmoke*. Much of the social science research on the effects of content proves little, especially when one considers the complexity of the problem and the difficulty of isolating the nature of the effect in an individual case. It is not always possible even to identify all the complicating forces. Thus, skepticism has arisen concerning the applicability of scientific research in resolving problems of violence. One common-sense authority asserts that the ordinary layman has no need of scientific detail to realize "that it can't be good for a child, or have no effect on him, if you give him a profusion of slugging, killing, torture, bleeding, branding and so on."[47] One may ask how it is reasonable to praise constructive television programs for giving constructive ideas, but deny that destructive scenes give destructive ideas. To paraphrase the late Bing Crosby, rather than depicting life as it is, the excessive-violence promoters are depicting life as it is going to be.

In 1971 *Saturday Review* made a content analysis of eight hours of Saturday children's prime time: they encountered "seven different kinds of pistols and revolvers, three varieties of rifles, three distinct brands of shotguns, six assorted daggers and stilletos, two types of machete, one butcher's cleaver, a broadaxe, rapiers galore, an ancient broadsword, a posse of sabers, an electric prodder, and a guillotine." Men, women and children were "shot by gunpowder, burned at the stake, tortured over live coals . . . repeatedly kneed in the groin, trussed and beaten."[48] Observers reported feeling no shock and being almost immune to seeing a human being in pain.

The fact remains that studies are too regional, too limited in coverage, and simply too tentative in general. Despite the apparent ease with which commentators, editors, advertisers, propagandists, politicians, administrators, preachers, educators and entertainers direct their messages over the mass media, the process is infinitely complex and specific facts that could advance the cause of reform are limited. Moreover, study findings can never be conclusive, since control groups are never fully representative, audiences are fluid and unobservable, short-term and long-term effects may not be separable, and it is difficult to determine whether a message or content is cause or effect.[49] A Harvard University authority, James Halloran, warns against researchers misleading themselves and others by an obsession with the elegant simplicity of one-dimensional analysis. On the question of whether violence on television affects society, *TV Guide* reports informed yet contrasting opinions, but concludes with a view that violence no longer serves any valid purpose.[50]

In addition, some research findings suggest the operation of a vicious cycle. The mass media, good or bad, reflect a society and personality which are, in turn, influenced or affected by the media. Media abuse and exploitation of sex, for example, has been called a symptom of a sexual sickness that already abounds in society, not its cause. To the sociologist and psychologist, the effect of the incidence of crime and sex on the mass media depends on the audience and the social framework of other interacting factors in which the content is received.

One paradox in some of the agitation for reform through research lies in the fact that the reformer often speaks with far less knowledge than the scientist offers him. A member of the Parent Teacher Association, the

American Civil Liberties Union, the American Legion, or other civic-minded organizations, for example, has been known to crusade before he or she has considered all of the factors. Sometimes the viewpoint and the mission are blurred by the person's distance from the problem. Elmo Roper and Associates in an opinion survey analyzed the attitudes of groups most concerned about the bad effects of television on children. They found that the concern came from (1) those who have no television or do not watch television, (2) those whose education level was grade school or lower, and (3) those with no children.[51] Further surveys may show that those who agitate for greater choice and more educational content do not themselves take advantage of already existing sober and varied offerings.

That constant undesirable content persists in the mass media cannot be denied. Audiences continue to attend to the unsavory on television, radio, screen, or in magazines and books. They show sustained interest in advertisements encouraging the purchase of countless nonessentials. But the actual correlation between the mass media display of controversial subject matter and the rise in crime and delinquency rates or growing cigarette and beer consumption will always be subject to a large measure of conjecture. Scientific research may, in fact, yield less usefulness than a movie critic who, in mingled despair and guarded optimism, asserted: "The people responsible for our mass entertainment could not possibly reach deeper into the ridiculous, the ugly and the pusilanimous than they have already gone—and that is surely a source of hope."[52]

A 14-year-old boy from Albion, Michigan hung himself in November 1973. He had been fascinated by rock-and-roll singer Alice Cooper whose performance featured a mock suicide. Motivated by questions of possible interrelationship between the mass media and educators, Howard Garner, professor in special education at Virginia Commonwealth University, wrote to the president of Warner Brothers records, raising the question of "responsibility in promoting and popularizing this destructive behavior," and pleading the abandonment of any idolization of suicide. The president of the media firm responded with allegations of demagoguery, stating that when a troubled boy takes his life, no industry can be held totally responsible.[53] Author Garner wrote up the correspondence with the media firm executive, concluding with a news wire service report from Calgary, Alberta as it appeared in the Atlanta *Constitution* in May 1974; it stated that a 14-year-old Calgary boy hanged himself while attempting to imitate Alice Cooper's mock hanging. An investigating jury called for immediate steps to ban programs of violence; a pathologist ruled out the possibility of suicide and said the boy apparently was indulging in a fad.

A news columnist described the game of "Dirty Harry" as played by two brothers in Columbus, Ohio. The film of the same name, shown during prime time on television, is a police drama which brought such box office success that it led to several sequels. Dirty Harry is a San Francisco cop who delights in taking the law into his own hands and firing his gun. The two boys had seen the movie Saturday night; Sunday morning, one lad with toy gun confronted the other with his father's .22 caliber derringer. The homicide division chief reported: "Seeing these things on television brings out the aggression in young people. Children . . . imitate the characters they see in TV." He referred to the FCC ban on cigarette and hard liquor advertising because of the hazards to health and asked whether the eighty-five murders per week on television are not also hazardous to health.[54]

In defending a 15-year-old boy on charges of first-degree murder in the shooting of his elderly next-door neighbor, Attorney Ellis Rubin tried to prove that the boy suffered from addiction to television violence and lost his sense of right and wrong. He claimed that the circumstances of the crime resembled episodes from the series Kojak and a Dracula movie watched the night before the murder.[55] Concerned with this kind of "absolute crisis state" of society, a government scientist with the Institute of Child Health and Human Development called for a 10-year ban on television and movie violence.[56]

The undulating discussion on whether or not media violence causes riots and murder, cigarette advertising induces smoking addiction, or beer promotion spreads alcoholism will continue. If the past record of individual freedom to apply the findings of social science research is any measure, it is unlikely that this will lead to a change in media content. A much more likely resolution, and perhaps the only one, will result from a reasonable discussion of value objectives in a healthy society, of give and take exchange between educators and media people. As psychologist Victor B. Cline stated concerning the scientists versus pornography: "While in a free society, some individuals may choose to immerse themselves in a pornographic milieu just as some people may choose to smoke excessively, in both cases these individuals should be made fully cognizant of the health hazards involved so they can make informed decisions."[57]

A weakness of many court arguments, reformist criticisms, and government actions lies in an open society's inherent resistance to those assertions which seem to propose censorship. The question, for instance, of whether or not scenes promoting violence, smoking or drinking are bad in themselves is not a closed one. Both history and the courts have made differing judgments of two violent acts. For example, neither the legal nor the medical profession can rule categorically or unanimously against the use of a mild stimulant or depressant. Smoking and drinking may be called unhealthy vices, but their promotion in the mass media reflects no more than accepted and, for many persons, hallowed examples and patterns of enjoyment, uplift and satisfaction. It is more tragic, of course, when the object of admiration is violence.

According to Western philosophy, that which is labeled bad today may be good tomorrow; the principle frequently applies to censorship. It is not unlike the rule of experimentation that asserts that a scientific truth is valid only until a firmer truth is discovered. John Stuart Mill wrote clearly of censorship in the essay, "On Liberty." It declares that to silence an opinion as untrue is to assume an unsupportable infallibility; to silence it as only partly true is equally foolish; the whole truth can be strengthened only through vigorous opposition from possible untruths. These arguments, often used to caution against interference from government, serve equally well as a deterrent to the censor.

Individual political, social or cultural organizations with the zeal to communicate to the masses intend a conversion to a single viewpoint. They promote a particular platform. Under the control of an interest group lacking the widest possible representation, the public mass media are likely to become detrimental to the principles of democratic freedom in the United States. Yet government has generally taken a hands-off view with regard to the media. Censorship of pornography may have been unsuccessful because it runs contrary to the desires of most people to censor. A big-city politician finds that there really are not any votes to be gained by banning X-rated movies and sex magazines. Court orders and police actions are deliberately left unenforced, leaving movie box offices free to communicate profanity and simulated sexual activity to hundreds of thousands weekly. For years the Supreme Court has been making rulings on obscenity, but it has not yet established a workable definition and may never be able to do so.

The individual who makes an extremely zealous mission of either criticism or censorship tends toward a peculiar imbalance, in that media failures and inadequacies become his livelihood. His function is to denigrate; his role is negative. He trains himself to seek the worst examples of content and to be blind and deaf toward all others; he is tempted to regard the mass media as totally evil unless they operate under his control or at least with his official approval. With the same selective use of memory, David Manning White states, "The culture Cassandras catalogue the worst examples of the mass media's efforts and consequently, generalize that Doomsday is surely near; otherwise, how could the mass media infest such kitsch and be deluded into thinking it nourishment?"[58] In yesteryear's golden ages, people are described as pursuing great thoughts of mankind and the noblest works of literature and the fine arts.

But, as Professor White has commented, such recitation lacks valid historical evidence and sacrifices accuracy for the sake of personal recollections. Moreover, he has observed, it avoids the bitter fact that fine music, ballet and literature did not deter Nazis from inhumanity to man and has not curbed other brutalitarians. It is a tragedy of the 1960s that a relatively few educated persons both on and off campus have sometimes lent leadership for brain-beaten, media-conscious hordes of organized destruction and nihilism.

One way to state the dilemma is as follows: A mass medium is a knife: in the hands of a maniac it destroys life; in the hands of a surgeon or educator it saves and restores.

Censorship as an operating principle is the most dangerous of reformist inclinations. Censorship is undesirable and unfair even when it is the device of a ruthless advertiser aiming to beat the competitor out of the listening, viewing and reading response of the great audience. Deliberately to suppress a book or program or recording is to threaten with annihilation the freedom of varying belief and expression and the right to sincere criticism that are basic in a democracy.

On the other hand, a rabid display of anticensorship adds nothing to the cause of mass media. The freedom to read, librarians and booksellers confess, is of little consequence when expended on the trivial.[59] In the early 1960s J. Edgar Hoover warned that many persons seemed unduly indulgent in attitudes toward crime, filth and corruption, much like judicial decisions that strain and stretch to give the guilty, not the same but vastly more protection than the law-abiding citizen.[60] Judge Curtis Bok held his nose with one hand as he protected nine unpleasant books against the charge of obscenity but he upheld with his other hand the right to free speech that the books represented.[61] The outspoken defender of trash, the degrading level of which he himself deplores, is not necessarily helping the fight against censorship.

One must also consider the ineffectiveness of criticism from lay people. Largely this ineffectiveness is their own fault—a result of their lack of reaction to the mass media. People who turn on the radio or television, visit the movie houses, or place coins in juke boxes are largely passive. The average individual reads a newspaper out of habit with little thought for its content. Most readers never entertain the thought of writing a letter to an editor. So argues the disillusioned classroom teacher: the public does not care if the media are vulgar. Nor did some students care, as the use of four-letter words in campus publications increased for a time to a degree of daily parlance, with the College Press Service of the U.S. Student Press Association ready to respond to any obscenity charges.[62]

No evidence, however, supports the view that most students endorse obscene language in private or in public or that the typical member of the mass audience always seeks and satisfies itself with mediocre content. People do not invariably choose the obscene or meretricious, let alone the cheap and tawdry. They are not incurably obsessed with violence, sensuality, alcohol, tobacco, cosmetics, speedy automobiles, automatic appliances. Neither sensationalism nor scandalmongering of any kind is natural fare. Media offerings that are restrained and moderate and that carry high cultural content do command large audiences.

Interestingly, some research has shown that the media are more effective when personal intermediaries—such as critics—exercise an influence. According to Elihu Katz and Paul Lazarsfeld, the media give information about and create a desire for the new, but public acceptance usually requires either personal persuasion or personal example by a respected opinion leader.[63] In other words, the most effective communications is a two-step flow coupling the public media and a face-to-face or word-of-mouth relay. Studies of voting behavior have shown that informal social relationships play a significant role in modifying the manner in which a given individual will act upon a message that comes to his attention via the mass media. In addition to adding information, the second step adds further interpretation.

The educator has blinded himself to the repeated opportunity to serve effectively in the second-step interventionist role of informer and interpreter of the media to the public. When student riots made headlines, he showed himself unable or unwilling to make the necessary personal association with both communicators and audiences. Apparently, educational reticence is governed by a certain personal, professional, and institutional security. Or is it insecurity?

It is possible that educators fit the description offered by Edgar Dale who wrote in the *Bulletin of the National Association for Better Radio and Television*: "The fatal weakness of all efforts to control the excesses and correct the errors of television in the United States is the attitude of people who think themselves untouched because they themselves never look at inferior programs or never see television at all. But there is no immunity—there is no place to hide."[64] This explanation of the ineffectiveness of criticism toward television can be applied to other mass media. It highlights the fact that, for better or for worse, the influence of the media is ubiquitous and virtually unaffected by the critics and doomsayers.

The people's insistence that the media need policing has, on occasion, met marked response, even if effective for only a brief period. A concatenation of murders in 1968 promptly triggered a national outcry against "excessive merchandising and dissemination of violence as a form of entertainment."[65] A fury of hasty revision of the topically and politically oriented films and recordings that had followed the assassination of President John F. Kennedy placed less emphasis on violence. Producers and writers at CBS, ABC and NBC television reexamined manuscripts, tapes and films that depicted violence for its own sake. Actors and actresses ran advertisements in Hollywood trade papers pledging their efforts against inordinate screen brutality. Comic pages of newspapers were scrutinized. The President assembled a National Violence Commission in the White House to undertake a penetrating search for the causes and prevention of violence. Later the Surgeon General of the United States issued a report generally interpreted as proof of the connection between violence on the screen and violence in young Americans.

If tied only to events, the efforts of criticism toward the media will bear little fruit. In fact, only one of seven questions before the President's Commission referred to the mass media. It is well concluded by Alberta Siegel in an article on "Communicating with the Next Generation" that the most convincing research about effects is that televised persons provide an example or a model for the viewers' behavior.[66] Her conclusion lends substance to Albert Schweitzer's remark: "Example is not the main thing in life—it is the only thing." Their comments favor the notable efforts of the comic magazine industry to develop the principle of self-regulation within the industry.

So long as reputable scholarly findings do not definitely prove that mass media presentations result in poor citizenship, undesirable habits, delinquent tendencies, or criminal acts—and such definite proof is unlikely—the mass communicator can and will continue to follow audience wishes very much as he has. So long as criticism of audience taste is obsessive and defensive, he need feel little insecurity. In the absence of positive alternatives, competing programs, and personal leadership, the criticisms of individuals and the investigations of interest groups or government will leave the mass communicator untouched. With impunity he may, if he chooses, cultivate either a "vast wasteland" or a "mass tasteland"; he may propagate confusion, distortion, frivolity and stupidity.

CONVICTIONS ABOUT THE AUDIENCE

The whimsical opinion a mass communicator holds regarding the audience may be the key factor in his success. As a member of the democratic citizenry, the communicator believes that he also is a member of the masses and his behavior is also a part of mass behavior. He can have his own private views, develop his own specialty, and reserve the right of choice among many alternative offerings of the media. He believes that individuals among the millions are just as interested in freedom of choice. He knows that an audience is influenced by what is offered but he does not believe that the audience is merely passive or that it is inferior in its tastes.

Two hundred million persons in a democracy cannot be wrong; the successful communicator tells himself that what they want or can be made to want is good. He may think of them as smaller audiences, such as housewife, teenager, laborer, or farmer, or he may adopt the ternary typology described by John Merrill and Ralph Lowenstein, journalism professors, in their book, *Media, Messages, and Men*.[67] They describe the "illiterates," or those disinclined to read, thus preferring movies, television and radio as perhaps 60 percent of all readers-listeners-viewers; the "pragmatists," or those who like to participate in society's varied activities as perhaps about 30 percent of the total mass audience; and the "intellectuals" as the estimated 10 percent who take issues and concepts seriously. Whatever the audience breakdown, the sub-groups each number in potential millions. Because the public medium itself is impersonal, he thinks of addressing Mr., Ms., Miss and Mrs. Individual for he knows that appreciation of the individual personality or self is basic. In the final analysis, it is upon each of them that the huge audiences depend. Acting in large numbers, it is they who give proof of a power exceeding that of the formal educator.

The public communicator is not unlike a person in live theater. He enjoys the response of audiences of all tastes and interests from a very large geographic region, potentially as large as the nation or the world. For decades, the media of print, radio, film and recordings carried his message afar; then satellite technology made television worldwide. The very thrill of participating in such an activity is part of the secret of mass media power.

The public media can be compared to a megaphone or a bugle. When a person finds one in his hands, he suddenly becomes aware of the power it will give his message. If he has no message, he seeks one. Then he believes it and performs it; he shouts it out for everyone to hear. He summons the greatest possible audience to come heed the message of his conviction. "Believe me, I know what I am talking about," he says. "Listen to my story! Do as I urge you! You will never regret it."

In his essay, "Self Reliance," Ralph Waldo Emerson stated: "To believe your own thoughts, to believe that what is true for you in your private heart is true for all men—that is genius."[68] Every successful communicator has a large measure of this genius. He has discovered for himself a truth so reliable and dependable that he believes with all his heart it must be true for others. He nurtures and universalizes his private truth until it grows into a sense of urgency to communicate. This dynamism has been seen in Ed Sullivan, Dick Gregory, Elizabeth Taylor, Norman Rockwell, H. L. Mencken, Sinclair Lewis, Marian Anderson, Leonard Bernstein, Walt Disney, Martin Luther King—or any number of past, present, and future performers, artists, writers, and media-conscious celebrities and opinion-builders.

It is true that monetary return and mounting profits form part of the incentive for building a large audience. Employees and consultants for a commercial venture obviously need compensation, and the manager or executive of a business or industrial firm requires profits. To this end, the sponsor, sustainer, publisher, and manufacturer select the communicating announcer, writer, artist, or performer for his or her ability to make every member of the audience believe that the product or idea is vital to his or her welfare. Like political revolutionaries, they have a gospel to preach, and they want converts and believers.

Successful commercial or ideological conversion caters to a mass audience. Media content that appeals only to self-conscious minorities divides the audience. For a time the Black Power movement held a strong hand over Black audiences, urging them to support "Black media" all in an effort to raise a long-suppressed awareness of and entitlement to equal status. Soon after, the mass media, primarily through television situation-comedy programs, aimed to convert audiences to homogeneity. Within a very few years, Blacks and Whites were seen together not only as neighbors and friends but also as man and wife, brother and sister, all to the delight of audiences.

A few years earlier the mass media had regarded the working class audiences as minority audiences who were both socially disruptive and commercially unattractive. The communicator faced a choice between accentuating the minority differences or attempting to mask differences in mass values and styles. The outcome was determined by the degree of the cohesion and isolation of a particular audience and the degree of opposition implicit in its minority values and goals. Audience numbers are what count, and a group of any promising size cannot be left out.

Would not any other approach to people as human beings be fraudulent? It is or should be almost inconceivable that a regular radio or television speaker could doubt the rightness of his message and still communicate. His is the demonstration of an aggressive approach grounded solidly on the foundations of a positive philosophy. Ambivalence is taboo. The communicators are at home with the theme of an old popular song, "Accentuate the positive, eliminate the negative, don't fool around with Mr. In-between."

The communicator does not pause long to consider whether his objectives are accepted. He settles for a reasonable certainty that they are, or that they can be made acceptable enough within the limits of legality to be "sold." He does not worry whether the content used to gain the effect appears to some as cheap, or whether he might become the target of hypocritical snipers. The communicator believes it is right enough. He shouts from the rooftops and adopts the most dramatic attention-getting techniques. He stands on his head, smiles irresistibly, and beckons: "Look, Ma, no hands."

In wielding an audience certain objectives must be met—to sell, to inform, to impress, to influence. With the broadest possible aims, the communicator tells himself: "What I write or say or perform is desirable or beneficial for someone, potentially for everyone, because it is part of the democratic culture—I never doubt this." Thus he studies, develops, and practices the big deal, the hard sell. He has combined a skill with a missionary purpose; he has, we realize, launched a crusade of conversions unparalleled in history.

The message of a mass medium is the work of a communicator and his group. The size and receptivity of the audience bear upon the intentions and viewpoint of the communicator and his choice or use of a medium. The nature of the effect is related to all of these factors and to the times, but it remains no less dependent upon the control and direction of the communicator and his group, and upon their integrity.

THE CULTURE OF THE MILLIONS

Not long ago *culture* was a term popularly used to denote the finer side of life, the high-brow things like classic novels and fine poetry, paintings and sculpture, and symphonies, operas and string quartets. It stood in sharp contrast to the cheap and low. In the framework of a modern democracy and among the majority of its members who comprise the masses, true culture embraces the sum total of what people are and have been. The communicator understands this.

Sociologists and anthropologists have helped to broaden the term *culture* to cover the whole of people's operating principles and behavior. It has been defined as (1) "the totality of products of social men, and a tremendous force affecting all human beings socially and individually";[69] (2) "the mass of behavior that human beings in any society learn from their elders and pass on to the younger generation";[70] (3) "all those artifacts, ideas, institutions, social ways, customs and the like which, taken in their totality, constitute the environment which man himself has made";[71] (4) "habits that are shared by members of a society."[72]

What was once seen as limited to the aristocratic and royal few or to specialized groups from lower classes (artists, for example, could be poor) has now become the common heritage of inspiration and misfortune, education and entertainment. Frank R. Leavis, author of

Education and the University, observed, concerning a wide newspaper circulation, that a psychological Gresham's Law operates to stimulate primitive feelings and impulses, first thoughts and established prejudices, rather than rational second thought.[73] Such a view is no longer appropriate. The secrets of the high-brow classroom graduate and the low-brow uneducated are now potentially knowable by people of all socio-economic levels. The modern mass media communicate the total culture, both high and low, both lasting and ephemeral, both good and bad.

· Some of the culture spirit of Walt Whitman's *Democratic Vistas* is being realized:

> I should demand a programme of culture, drawn out, not for a single class alone, or for the parlors or lecture-rooms, but with an eye to practical life, the west, the working-men, the facts of farms and jack-planes and engineers, and of the broad range of the women also of the middle and working strata, and with reference to the perfect equality of women, and of a grand and powerful motherhood. I should demand of this programme or theory a scope generous enough to include the widest human area. It must have for its spinal meaning the formation of a typical personality of character, eligible to the uses of the high average of men—and *not* restricted by conditions ineligible to the masses. The best culture will always be that of the manly and courageous instincts, and loving perceptions, and of self-respect—aiming to form, over this continent, an idiocrasy of universalism. . . .[74]

In the latter half of the twentieth century, universalism would relate to pop culture, significant not only because millions of people like it and spend much time and money on it but also, as one author stated, because of the intoxicating dynamism of its vitality and immediacy.[75] It is a universal, a part of our lives as most of us sing the same songs about love and heroism and the solutions to social problems and the same refrain about what we wear and eat and do. It helps us to better understand ourselves as intermeshed within a total culture. Just as public communicators use pop culture as a great middle ground, educators do well to explore its potential. Writing in the *English Journal*, Jesse Hine referred to the explosion of media and print and the desire to make classes exciting and meaningful. She pleads for the use of popular culture in the classroom.[76]

Culture in a democracy represents the truth or near-truth of its members. It is that which all or most of the population freely agree upon. The action of a hundred-million persons exposed to a variety of alternatives in all areas of life largely creates the world in which the other hundred-million live. In their article, "Mass Communication, Popular Taste, and Organized Social Action," Paul Lazarsfeld and Robert Merton assert that the mass media serve primarily to reenforce the prevailing culture patterns, and that the very conditions that made the mass media effective tend to maintain rather than to change the going social and cultural structure.[77] One can acknowledge this, but must, by no means preclude the powerful role directed toward change by individual communicators imbued with convictions.

The communicators and operators of the mass media are committed to the serious business of making and transmitting the broad culture, almost more so than is expected by educators. They are "acculturizers"— to use the sociological term. As leading acculturizers, the media people exercise a large measure of control over the effects of the mass media on the welfare of all of us. The transmission of cultural patterns, what is and what ought to be, has become a media mission and function without society ever intending that this vital role be transferred from the domain of public education. To an incredible degree, the media *make* the mass culture one that carries both conservative and liberal qualities.

THE EDUCATOR AND CULTURE

Culture transmission on a mass scale is, of course, hardly the innovation of media people. For generations, educators have led the way; they have been the tastemakers, the innovators, the preservers and the disseminators. For centuries, the schools channelled students into various subject areas in which the culture was transmitted. The relationship between educators and culture has been symbiotic. Culture cannot thrive without a structure for education, and education cannot exist without culture. In the most general terms, the campus at all levels acculturizes as it disseminates basic knowledge and teaches the productive skills for maintaining life. This is the task to which society specifically assigns it.

The culture of the schools has ranged not only from the basic four R's of reading, writing, arithmetic and religion but also to the classical languages, literature, art and music. The transmission of cultural ideas has long been part of a noble calling for hundreds of thousands of teachers. (Their dedication of the early twentieth century in the classroom still exists.) The teacher came to know the problems and ambitions of young people and followed their careers with interest. From learning, travel and community services, the teacher's experiences were rich. His economic status improved over the years. He has traditionally enjoyed a position of respect in the community and a place of leadership among local gatherings of many kinds.

But in recent decades all has not gone smoothly. In fiction, the teacher may be a bit like a beloved Mr. Chips or Mr. Novak, but in truth, mass society no longer sees him as a star. For example, on the television program "Person to Person," chaired for six of its seven years by the education-minded dean of broadcast commentators, Edward R. Murrow, only four educators were represented in 480 appearances, in contrast to 368 or 76 percent entertainers (including journalists).[78] Grayson Kirk, former president of Columbia University, said: "Education occupies a curiously ambiguous position in the affections of the American people. . . . If our people have a profound faith in education, they do not have an equally profound faith in our educators. . . . The scholarly cap and gown is still the cartoonist's favorite symbol for something which is impractical, even foolish."[79]

On an unfortunately wide scale, college and university teachers play their role either up to the point of abstracted intellectualism or down to the density of a mere occupation. With pitiful frequency, parents have steered their children away from seriously considering the vocation of teaching as a first choice, lending new fire to the old Socratic adage that "one who can, does; one who merely knows, teaches." Respect for the educator is on less than a grand scale in large measure because educators have overlooked the fact that curriculum includes the totality of the century's culture and the breadth of its influence. The English critic, Lancelot Hogben, conceded, "Having found 'common things at last,' the last insult which I would offer the worker is the culture of our universities."[80]

While educators hide from the fullness of their task, the mass media of public communications—the ubiquitous television, radio, movies, records, newspapers, magazines and paperback books—are filling their role as chief formulators of culture. Robert M. Hutchins considered the influence of magazine publisher Henry Luce to be two to twenty-five times as great as that of the President of the University of Chicago. He wrote: "If you take all the radio and television stations of this country, if you take the newspapers and the magazines and roll them up together, and ask yourself what the influence of these institutions is upon the American character as opposed to the educational system, I think you would admit that the mass media have carried the field."[81]

The public media have the unequivocal goal of an even more massive audience. The educator's reaction to their success in disseminating culture and influencing behavior is generally a combination of speciously misdirected overconcern or ridiculously inept underconcern. More often than not, their reactions contain none of the proven techniques nor the energy and focus of the mass communicator. They are frequently negative. The humane or moral cause in many college courses is a void into which rush the banal and the narrow, the sordid and the cruel, the hopeless and the sullied from the mass media. It is little wonder that seeds of social unrest found the campus to be the best place in which to germinate and that the college became a human desert devoid of human emotions.

Writing in the mid-1950s Paul L. MacKendrick was one university professor who seemed to understand the problem. His remarks are incisive and sobering: ". . . humanistic scholars have allowed a vacuum to develop in the mass media, into which have rushed elements which we regard as vulgar . . . . We freeze before reporters, despise radio and television, deplore Hollywood and the Reader's Digest and insist, in our opinion quite rightly, that Great Books are the only civilized visual aids. This, of course, pleases us in a minority, and, as William Riley Parker has put it, we think the minority is always right, and the smaller the righter."[82]

In the name of intellectualism, an educator may assert that he cannot stand the callousness of radio or television for more than a few moments at a time, or that the weekly picture magazines are all for the degraded, lowly and common reader. In his deep concern for values, he may feel an impulse to scream at the sight and sound of most mass media content. His irritation may climax in an emotional outburst or a form of reverse snobbery against media success, which is likely to add only disrespect for his profession.

One oft-stated folly of the critic's undue discomfiture lies in the fact that there is no physical pressure on the individual to expose himself to the media. In not doing so, he need fear no repressive or preventive measures through legislation or government action. "No political or public reaction, nothing," writes the Director General of UNESCO, "forces me to buy that silly newspaper or that childish magazine; nothing obliges me to listen to that stupid radio programme or to watch that vulgar or vapid show."[83] The fact is that the content has been legitimized by social custom and economic needs which are a part of all of us, making the only proper censorship the option of audience members to turn the knob or in a poll most of the people stated they were against violence, but that they were willing to break away from their favorite television violence long enough to respond to the survey.

The point at issue is not that the public audiences and the individuals within them are more violent or virile, more smoked or soaked. While statistics may show a positive correlation between attention to mass media offerings and the purchase of guns and contraceptives, number of gun killings and sex crimes, the alarming issue is that unrestrained public communications can potentially make millions of people do things they do not wish to do. Spellbound, people prostitute themselves into gripping habits and expectations that they acknowledge to be undesirable. They begin to demand what they do not want, and that is schizophrenic. They act as if government and the media are joined in conspiracy. They lose their true freedom not only to say but also to think, not only to choose but also to listen to their own best judgment. Their schizophrenic behavior is narcotized.

Unless their education has been truly liberal and their inclinations are humanitarian, educational personnel are as susceptible as others to practices that are a contradiction to their teaching. An unfortunate habit is to point an accusing finger at majority-rooted mass media and other enterprises for their sham and profiteering and therefore to discard them from serious concern. The educator might well address a few questions to himself and to his profession. Is he free and innocent of narrowly vested interests in his occupation, his department, his specialized ware? Have those in charge of campus public relations, as Francis Pray suggests, tried a moratorium on "weeping and wailing about the plight of higher education," and the substitution of genuine person-to-person relations?[84]

Are there college teachers who look on culture-oriented, that is, liberal-general, courses as sheer drudgery necessary to support a handful of advanced students and a personal project of specialized research? Do any decry extension or continuation programs? Do any seek the easiest path to the paycheck and manage to waste time en route? Are there teachers whose interest in their cause is mere lip service? Could there be any academicians who calm themselves with the thought that they have tenure while the media people do not? If so, can selfish motivations behind any of these possibilities among college teachers be termed anything more virtuous or commendable than the commercialism of the mass communicator?

The simplest rules of salesmanship and advertising suggest that a salesman can or should get nowhere by withdrawal, by saying what merchandise is not, or by deriding his competitors. Advertising would not have its success if it were not persistent and positive. Similarly, educators cannot communicate effectively to the millions when they blankly criticize the popular taste, draw a wall of smug superiority around themselves, engage in wild controversy over objectives, and take sharply divided sides in battles between "Educators" and "educators." They only reinforce a popular impression that they have something which they think everyone ought to have, but which no one really wants.

Laws already exist to protect people from the exploitation of commercialism, but what protects them from education? Educators must gain support of public opinion for content that is equally or more appealing than mass media. Young people for the most part are resilient and of fundamentally good nature, craving more emphasis on honest human relations and social improvement. They may be better equipped than adults to withstand, ward off, and digress from demoralizing influences.

Either as rabid censor or as rabid anticensor, an educator is out of place. The key adjective here is *rabid* in the sense that either extremist position is irrational, unreasonable and intolerant, representing or attempting to silence opposing viewpoints. In considering the school to be a comprehensive communications medium, educators may place themselves in unfair competition for the attention and loyalty of students by attempting to eliminate all complicating mass media content. In justifying an action as good and democratic, the narrow critic frequently has in mind one which seems good and democratic *to him*. The educator who spends his time exclusively on the censorial crusade neglects the objectives and content of his own offerings. He may even lack the time or will to present them effectively.

Any educator who loathes or fears the task of dealing with millions of citizens of all ages and in all occupations, who believes that only a very few of the millions can love literature, history, science, mathematics and art, belittles his profession as much as a physician would if he believed that health is possible and desirable only for a very few people. He presumes a hopeless view long before he has made genuine efforts; he gives up before really trying. Critic Gilbert Seldes wrote in *The Public Arts*: ". . . the defect of all attempts so far to influence the mass media has been an almost snobbish dislike for them and an exaggerated fear. We have to recognize a possible danger. We have no right to panic in front of an imaginary one."[85] There is no need for a chronic mediaphobia.

A teacher's lack of concern with mass media frequently coincides with a lack of interest beyond a prescribed textbook or teaching method. To an unfortunate degree, the teaching-learning process of pupils after the class hour, or of the numerous citizens who are not pupils, is only of an ironic academic nature. A University of Delaware professor urged: "The changing character of our undergraduate enrollments should be a challenge to carry the torch of humanistic learning into byways where it has never shone before, and the 'electronic gadgetry' which so many of us fear should provide vehicles, not stumbling blocks on the road to wisdom."[86] For Wilbur Schramm, "the mass media are but a bridge between schools and community."[87]

For the educator, the fight should not be with commercialism or mass opinion or censorship. The issue is neither the viewpoint of an interest group nor the findings of a scientist that a mass medium offering has harmful or anti-social effect. The crime is not violence or sensuality in large doses nor any popular vice or sweeping fad. All is not bad; all is not good. Neither scientific experiment nor confused emotions, censorship nor irresponsible freedom, are very helpful in the cause of better content and more wholesome effect. The damning of individuals or groups for malicious wrongdoings accomplishes nothing. The task is to seek out the interpersonal causes of the present dilemma and proceed from there to propose solutions.

While the effect of public communications is the result of several forces, the message itself, its interest and content, and the enthusiasm and conviction behind it are, to recapitulate, largely within the province of the communicator. He controls much of the effect. If he is truly smitten with a noble purpose, as are most educators, if he has a contagious enthusiasm and he is fearless and positive in the face of criticism and competition, his mass audiences will receive worthwhile, beneficial content.

The issue for the responsible member of the teaching profession is his concern with meeting the vital objectives of both content and audience. The answer, thus, lies in a willingness to cooperate with mass communications both in the public process and through personal encounter. Stepped up to the competing pace of the other media, the formula runs as follows: The teacher, as communicator and as guide, utilizing and influencing the full range of liberal arts and general studies, communicating publicly to millions of the mass media audiences and personally to thousands in the classroom and the community, could enjoy impressive effects. William D. Boutwell, Director of Scholastic Book Services, implores the teachers of English "to take a much larger responsibility for preparing youth to cope successfully with the ever-increasing fallout of mass communication."[88]

The author of this book outlines the challenge for all teachers, as well as for all communicators and other citizens. While urgent as well as universal, it is not one that requires the adopting of any elaborate or pretentious program of action. No thorough rewriting of textbooks, reconstruction of buildings, establishment of new organizations, development of research, nor revision of teacher preparation is called for. That is the beauty of the thesis. All that is required is a professional attitude that will embrace the total educational potential of the public media, which are after all sister media to the classroom for general-liberal curricula. All that is needed is a realistic reaffirmation of the widely proclaimed liberal arts-general studies objectives and an enthusiasm for making them effective for the modern world.

Reactions to the idea of greater cooperation between educators and public communicators have varied widely. On one hand, persons as different as an English professor and an advertising man have sworn that the two functions have nothing in common and that any sharing of ideas and offerings at present is purely accidental. Other persons, including an academic dean and a band leader, have stated that they have everything in common and that the common bond will grow. We can only say that it must.

The solution is more significant than anything else anyone has dabbled at so far. The group of seven mass media, communicating almost simultaneously and instantaneously to millions, is far more than a mere technical appurtenance to society. It is far more practical than a new way of writing the history of Western Civilization or an excuse for philosophizing on social change and determinism. A solution can be no secular prayer to technology or dulling incantation designed to quell fears of the machines that make media. Laissez-faire is not the solution.

Left alone to develop as they have, the mass media will only become more paltry and commercial; education more vocational, ingrown, vested, withdrawn, elite. In cooperation, they will foster a unique opportunity: educator and communicator together will become more liberal and responsive, more self-critical and outgoing, more constructive and aware. When either force curses the other as an irritant or disregards its potential, it increases the possibility of both remaining as they presently are, as irritable and remote from each other as they have been.

An educator's leadership can harness the power of the mass media to effect major social, political and economic improvements among people. With his participation, there is little danger that the communications revolution can lead to a race of silent men whose thoughts and actions are governed by the puppets of press and electronics. As the myth of trying to isolate effects vanishes into a proper irrelevancy, the possibility of unaffected mastery of the mass media rises above the horizon. A new educational and communications era begins.

7

MEDIA POWER AND CAMPUS POWER IN STRIDE

How differently schools might have developed in many communities if modern networks of public communications had existed a century ago. Political and social isolations and dissensions would have taken other forms. Human relations might have been a strange blend of mediacy and loneliness. The levels of world literacy and, presumably, international understanding would be much higher.

Books have long been intimately associated with schooling, but if they and their mass distribution had not been invented, classroom education might have rested in "listening and seeing" instead of "reading, writing, and arithmetic." As it is, the longer established world of print remains irreplaceable as a foundation for other media. The author has earlier written of its being the indispensable environment for teaching and learning.[1] At least in the capacity of libraries to mobilize around, rather than succumb to, the new technologies, Arthur Schlesinger writes that Gutenberg is very much alive.[2] Even in the fact of computerization, the printed word grows in strength and competes with television, radio, movies, and recordings. The media's combined challenge to the educator, which increases almost daily, will encourage or enforce vast changes in the schools of tomorrow. What the changes will be cannot be known with certainty. Yet their trend and temper are already apparent, and no educator can ignore them.

OBJECTIVES AND VALUES

A healthy society in today's world requires basic continuing education for every citizen. A people or nation may enjoy representation in government, diversity in religion, variety in communications, free enterprise in business, and harmonious labor-management in industry, but none of these can last, or grow, without the promotion of a liberal-general, democratic understanding among all citizens.

Education must be advertised and promoted. If it is to be effective for a democracy, the false dividing lines within it must be erased. That implies a more relevant task than what occurs when each level isolates itself from the others. For example, except as it may be necessary in modern society in order to gain public support for funding a completely separate philosophy, legitimacy and professionalism just for adult education would seem unfortunate.[3] The sharp lines between educational levels should never have been drawn in the first place. It is strange that anyone should ever question that education is a continuing necessity for all citizens, and that it must be widely available. Education is more than a few years of high school or college. It is more than an exclusive function of any professional educator. It is more than a textbook or a program or any set of books or of programs. Education can be simultaneously informative and entertaining, but, as philosopher Alfred North Whitehead has commented, like any work that is "transfused with intellectual and moral vision," it can also be turned into a joy, triumphing over its weariness and its pain."[4]

Governments of other countries have demonstrated the effectiveness of cooperation between the educational system and the mass media. Dictatorial rule over both of these revolutionary forces, of course, is tragic, but sharp differences in their functions mean an unstable society. The need is for an environment where, by joining education and media in partnership, there is also the promise of freedom, equality, and justice on which the health of a democratic nation feeds. These same principles are central to the liberal arts objectives that help people to assimilate information, think clearly and evaluate critically. Nurtured with simplicity and tolerance, these tenets are in turn fundamental to successful communications between campus and populace.

The school system in the United States fulfills a commendable role of educating through the classrooms. It is the chief source of supply in the form of workers and research for the leaders who sustain the growth of the nation's institutions. At the same time, the formal system is gravely limited in the direct influence that it can have. It communicates education largely during childhood and youth, a few hours a day, a few days a week. It measures educational intake by credit hours, semesters, grades, diplomas and degrees. Over the objections of educators themselves, when these measures are inflated and abused as symbols of educational achievement and effectiveness, good students rebel and some drop out, setting a poor example for others.

The quantitative aims of colleges and universities should continue to be more students in more commencement exercises on campus, necessitating advance planning to accommodate the enrollment. At the same time, the objectives should expand to make all citizens aware of what is frequently called the commencement concept. It means that for all citizens of all ages in a dynamic democracy, education is and must be an ever recurrent beginning. If, as is often said, the future of the country lies in education, the professional educator has a role that cannot stop short of national and international impact. Now, more than ever before, an expanded role is a possibility—indeed it is a necessity.

Vastly larger in scope and not at all concerned with education's traditional symbols, the mass media of public communications can and do transmit manifold and random kinds of education to everyone above cradle age. They cut across audience differences of occupation, school level, age, sex, race and location. To a far greater extent than is possible on a campus, the mass media achieve full democratic coverage for all possible audiences.

The demands on a free citizenry make it plain that, after school hours or after school years, no one is ever free from the need for orientation in the knowledge and practice of the high ideals of humanity. It may be said that those not privileged to have had much formal schooling are in gravest need of liberalizing knowledge, and that those who have received diplomas have the gravest obligations to practice liberal ideals. Formal schooling in the goals and principles of democracy must be accompanied by a consciousness of a lengthened time and a broadened inclusiveness of popular education. The subject of democracy in the curriculum embraces all of people's educable nature, with the emphases on individuality, values and change. A school is among the institutions for making the members of society sometimes conformist and conservative in various areas and independent and outspoken on occasion in others. In submitting to this process without sacrifices of either dignity or importance, the formal school curricula also respect the lasting values of mankind and the rich variety in every human being.

This variety is wide: there is humanity in all of its mediocrity and self-satisfaction, the results of yielding to the grinding gears of curricular conformism, the people who have received the degree and forgotten its substance. In contrast, there is humanity realizing itself through the habits of higher learning; the degree remains a secondary consideration. There is humanity with the patience, the persistence, and the romance for enlarging and developing the bravest of its nature.

Man's widely varied nature seeks the values of knowledge, wisdom and well-being. The tools of the common life—reading, writing, speaking and mathematics—are developed from the early grades onward, along with an orientation in the history, geography, arts and sciences of our culture. High school and college offer a quadrangular plan of studies: (a) the natural and physical sciences, (b) the social sciences, (c) the humanities, and (d) the health and training of the body.

Knowledge of school subjects is sharpened considerably by exposures outside the classroom and after graduation. These are the periods when the modern mass media communicate not only the "what is" (in terms of demand) but also much of the "what ought to be" (in terms of value). In combination, formal and informal education makes an individual complete, capable of understanding and appreciating the largest possible breadths of living. Whatever the vocational calling, there is always hope for the bold vision beyond the usual and the immediate, a glimpse almost of the ultimate in human achievement.

A TRIPLE RESPONSIBILITY

A person in possession of a liberal and general education regards it as necessary to be both learned and taught. It is also something to be practiced. Implicit in the best hope of education is the expectation that each citizen can and will be imbued with an enthusiasm for liberal learning, which will spread to others. The example set by a good learner is inseparable from the example set by a good teacher; each will mirror the other and both will practice what they learn and teach.

Student teaching is a course taught in colleges and universities that offer practical experience to a teacher trainee. It is one aspect of his or her learning and professional preparation that has not come under serious attack. In student teaching the candidate for a degree or certificate in teaching demonstrates the most important objective of the course work, namely the ability to bring to others the subject matter he or she has learned. In the school of law, a law student practices his or her knowledge in a mock court; in medical school the young medic interns in a hospital. In many other careers, a student's learning is enhanced by practice.

The difference between student-learning and teacher-training has been tediously and foolishly overworked. The methods may vary from such extremes as laissez-faire, progressivist, open or nondirected teaching to the traditional one of assign-study-recite, but distinctions among methods have little relevance or value for education in a world shaped by public communications. Student and faculty apathy, no less than inordinate student and faculty demands, campus demonstrations and riots, are clear evidence demonstrating gaps between the strata of academe and between theory and practice.

It does little or no good for liberal arts students to learn humanitarian principles and then not teach them to their associates. It is an even greater folly and affront if graduates assume administrative positions and then practice illiberal principles. For to practice examples of illiberality and irresponsibility in human affairs is, in effect, to teach these ills. In brief, with the freedom to learn comes the responsibility to teach. With the freedom to teach comes the responsibility to learn.

Frequently a college instructor reminisces: "I learn more in teaching a subject than I ever learned from merely taking the course in school." This truth merits the widest possible curricular use. In an article titled "Human Relations in Education," Ernest O. Melby wrote, "The school of education in the future is going to assume that everybody in the community is an educator. Everybody is a teacher. He can't escape being a teacher. Since he is a teacher, the best thing to do is to equip him to be a teacher."[5]

Professional teaching in the future will increasingly distinguish between authoritarianism and authoritativeness, between commanding a student through dogma and guiding a student by example. In his book, *Experiment in Education*, William E. Hocking refers to the inadequacy of formulating ideal and laudable principles unless they are closely related to the habits of nations, including one's own.[6] The inadequacy also applies when these principles are incompletely related to the mass media content and effect that largely govern individual habits. Learning to teach successfully is learning to lead toward futures near and far. Leadership must also be educative, or it does not lead onward.

No realm of teachers that sets an uneducated example can expect an educated performance from students. In his book about the relationship of the university to democracy, Norman Foerster wrote that the "instructor and advisor of youth, the liberal teacher, is usually successful in exact proportion as he is himself exemplary. What he is—in mind, personality, character—his students will tend to become."[7] If education means greater use and application of reason, finer morals and ethics, deeper understandings, and more responsible and active citizenship, it is important that, in all of these meanings, the educated person be himself, in the best sense, that is, a self worthy of conscious or unconscious imitation. It is important to remember that the educated are made up of learning teachers and teaching learners.

The commitment to teach and to communicate through the mass media is one with liberal learning and humanitarian practice. The responsibilities and privileges of a professional teacher and a classroom learner in a free society, it is now obvious, extend much further than formal instruction, assigned reading, or campus-sponsored electronics. They are among the most imposing and ongoing in all human endeavors. None is on a grander scale.

REALISM AND THE CURRICULUM

Knowledge increases in complexity far more rapidly than the span of an individual's life can be lengthened to appreciate it. Clearly people need to consider every possibility of transmitting and absorbing the fullest measure of knowledge. They must also scrutinize how far from "realistic" experience many traditional classroom assignments are. It is not a question of taking sides with John Dewey, who insisted that students say "we have experiences" rather than "we know," for he also believed that one's life-style must be responsible. His words highlight the need to align education vibrantly closer to the media world.

Some knowledge and behavioral patterns are so simple that they are taken care of by the natural processes of walking, talking, listening and identifying persons and objects close to daily life. Most skills of observation and discrimination begin and continue without formal schooling. A curriculum pioneer, Franklin Bobbitt, may have oversimplified this by assuming that "only those abilities which are so complex that they are not sufficiently developed through the normal processes of living" should be included in a system of schools.[8] Yet, his statement presumes that much important learning goes on outside the classroom. This learning, it bears repeating, includes the messages of public communications.

Emphasizing the teacher's task of transmitting the best knowledge of others 1,500 years ago, St. Augustine asked: "Who is so foolishly curious as to send his son to school to learn what the teacher thinks?"[9] Still earlier, Seneca bemoaned: "We learn, unfortunately, the lessons not of life, but of the schools."[10] Today both of these ancient men of wisdom might join in opening the educational system to the use of the liberal-general content of the mass media, which will, of course, also include the thoughts of many teachers. If teachers would not be educators in the full meaning of the word, then let any among them change the title of their occupation to "classroomist" or "classroom technician."

Obviously no human being can or should "live it all," as life is sometimes misinterpreted. Many liberalizing and generalizing experiences are indirect, undetermined and unplanned. The degree of vicariousness and vagueness, however, can be considerably lessened. The richness, fullness, depth and breadth of experience, while still "at safe distance" and within the boundaries of propriety, can in fact be communicated by skillful co-ordination of curriculum and mass media content and effect.

Among today's educators, there has been a glowing enthusiasm for the realism that modern audiovisual devices can bring to the classroom. Much of the automated help is excellent; more of it is first of all elaborate. The Educational Facilities Laboratories, funded by the Ford Foundation to help colleges in their campus physical planning, lavishly publicized its endeavors to set up fully furnished centers of electronic hardware. Commercial firms offer a variety of computer-based instructional systems. By merely looking for a trademark with the phrase, "media or modal technology," educators can order an array of gadgetry such as they have never before known. Sometimes as capriciously as the rebellious remarks of students and bandwagon teachers, the contrast with traditional methods has been colorfully expressed as in the following example:

> The dull droning of meaningless repetition, the regurgitation of undigested facts, the monotony of endless drill is really cruel, but, unfortunately, not unusual punishment of the children who go hopefully to school. We have at hand the means to enrich every aspect of school experience. Through the use of modern devices such as motion pictures, radio, television, field trips, projected pictures and recordings, the classroom can be an exciting, interesting and challenging place in which to live and work.[11]

At times, with seemingly limitless financial aid, the promoter of audiovisual technology in the classroom lets his imagination run almost to the outer limits of manufactured episodes and pseudorealism. At one university, a professor's efforts at combining movies, triple slide projectors, sounds, and smells all in the convenience of one room were admiringly described as follows:

> We had projected before us a color slide showing a distant view of a cathedral of ancient Europe. As the slides increased in scale and the accompanying music increased in tempo, we moved closer and closer to the cathedral. Shortly we were confronted on three screens with the details of the doorways . . . we were looking at what might be not only the front of the cathedral but the sides as well . . . . Possibly fifteen seconds elapsed before we "entered" the cathedral. Light fanned in from its windows, and once more we had the feeling that we were inside this ancient edifice. The scale was there, the atmosphere had been created, and the appropriate organ music was heard. As we sat in this atmosphere, we were ever conscious of the incense—it had been carefully prepared and blown through the room by means of fans.[12]

Another teacher tried an intermedia approach to show film and its interrelationships with society. After reading the following description of an incredible effort to maintain attention by utilizing media equipment, one is left wondering why the subject matter itself and the instructor do not hold more appeal:

> Stereo music is playing . . . as students arrive. Slow at first, it gets wilder as starting time nears. Tapes, color slides, films and "mind-blowing" music are used throughout the lectures. Any name or concept of special note is flashed on one of four screens. If the class gets too comfortable, a Sousa march or some calisthenics wake it up.[13]

Approaches to realism through the media in the classroom may or may not become more commonplace. Creative arts departments teaching music, painting, sculpture, drama, film, radio and television have much to offer other departments. Even with student labor and talent, however, the cost of extravagant efforts such as the foregoing is prohibitive in most campus budgets. They are more economically suited to World's Fair extravaganzas, or to world travel courses. Moreover, such efforts on campus are unnecessary and unreasonable, except on a modest scale, as workshop experiments and aids for teaching special skills. It is paradoxical that an overemphasis on bringing media, mechanical, audio visual techniques into the classroom coexists with a professional failure to explore the commercial mass media as a viable and money-saving adjunct to the classroom.

The simple factors in the paradox bear emphasis. The most luxurious commercial productions—a hundred million dollars worth of communication equipment—are within reach almost without cost. The conditions and curricula under which students and other citizens learn and can be encouraged to learn are already at hand. Most of the population is not in school, and even students enjoy more hours of exposure to the mass media than to the classroom. In terms of sheer quantity, the average person today learns much more from the mass media than he or she learns from any other institution, perhaps more than from all others combined.

The use of audiovisual and other mechanical aids in classroom instruction should certainly be encouraged. When closed circuit television, radio, recordings, films, magazines and paperbacks, including comic books, are carefully interwoven with course objectives and lesson plans, they make for more pleasant hours at school. It is gratifying to the enlightened parent when a child returns from a day at school to report the enjoyment of geography or of music televised or broadcast specifically for a given class, of science as presented by the printed word as well as in the laboratory, of arithmetic as animated in a film, or of physical education made more rhythmic with a recording. Yet, in a mass media world, it is a sign of decided progress when the same child at home has learned to expect wholesome and educational quality from evening and weekend television, radio and stereo, at the neighborhood movie, and in newspapers and magazines.

Those who are specialists in the use of audiovisual techniques and the printed word in the instructional process in school and college, whether they call themselves experts in learning resources or librarians, can find one of their greatest challenges in helping the student to transfer to his or her world of "media for the millions" the same association between educationally enjoyable content and audio, visual, or printed media that he has experienced in the classroom. They should help us answer the question of why this carry-over wanes as the child matures. The claim of greater sophistication is a poor answer. It is deplorable that by the time a student reaches college, the division between classroom media and public mass media is complete. It is schizophrenic, as an earlier chapter asserts, when the typical student thinks of the classroom as educational, and thus hopelessly dull, and of public mass media as non-educational, and thus enjoyable and highly promising.

THE ABUNDANCE OF EDUCATION

Despite the danger that critics imply when they speak of yellow journalism, commercial television and degrading movies, the mass media comprise not only a vital backdrop to education for the high school and college student but also the most convenient resource for any continuing seeker of a liberal-general education. In this search, of course, the media should not be the only progenitor or custodian of his ideas and ideals, rather, the learner becomes aware of their educational abundance as a fully stocked supermarket of educational wares for the open-minded yet discriminating customer.

Even the skeptic is stunned by abundance of content on the media. They convey a full range of life's tensions and releases, its restrictions and freedoms, its tragedies and comedies, its griefs and joys, indeed, of all the sights and sounds and other sensations in the world, of the dimensions of the universe. Violence, vulgarity and undesirable habits are there, but so are gentility and love, idealism and character. The media communicate culture, generally orient people in their society, influence their attitudes and values, and entertain in ways that add to knowledge and understanding. The scope and challenge of the media are at least equal in breadth to those of classroom curricula.

The question is how the pursuer of a liberal arts education is to select from and organize the outpouring of the media. For a liberal-general education *is* structured, and its contents are of more than trivial or compartmentalized significance. Indeed, the role of instruction is to pull together the valuable and the diverse, to see the forest as well as the trees. Some offerings are clearly labeled as educational. A weekly television magazine indicates with an asterisk the programs that will be meaningful supplements to studies in such areas as literature, history, science, the arts and contemporary affairs. Helpful as this may be, the self-respecting aspirant to education rightfully considers a label rather irreverent and unreliable.

Print and recording media offer answers to the questions of what education is, where it can and should aim, and what it can and should include. Newspapers and news magazines summarize the remarks of educators and civic leaders on the theme of educational direction. They also carry reviews of books on education. Other guidance may be had from such national magazines as *Newsweek*, *Saturday Review*, *Harpers*, *Atlantic* and *The Reader's Digest*, especially in the issues near the opening of the school year and during commencement in May or June. Record catalogues list recordings of educational spokesmen giving purpose to learning and study. From the same sources one can learn how to approach the traditional content groupings that have proved meaningful and satisfactory for a liberal-general education: the humanities, the social studies, the physical and natural sciences and health and physical education.

These groups offer an effective academic framework and discipline and have done so for decades. They have roots in centuries of tradition. While under attack by self-styled innovators and certainly open for revision, they will by no means disappear in the foreseeable future. Knowledge and learning in each of these fields are today a part of the daily environment of everyone. Anyone can realize their benefits for himself through simply analyzing and recording the otherwise unconnected bits of culture or quasi-education of mass communication, which one educator refers to as a dilemma. The first step is to attempt what social scientists call a content analysis of the media.[14]

Experts in content analysis have published studies of the frequency, types and trends of films, radio, television, comics, newspapers, textbooks, best-sellers and magazines. One procedure is to classify the content under various carefully-defined categories. An educator in a particular field of study occasionally makes an outline of assignments involving mass media other than books. Periodicals frequently carry editorial overviews of the worlds of broadcasting, filming, publishing and recording.

But any general survey, assigned outline, or periodical summary is soon dated. A personal assessment is much more timely, accurate and pertinent. Because a liberal education in particular is acquired through one's own experience, the impact of writing, recordings, and programs follows a different pattern for each member of their audiences. Much less reward comes from reading a comprehensive outline made by an expert than from personal effort by the educational aspirant in his own organized, goal-oriented fashion.

Each day, in this media approach to continuing education, the student takes stock of his contacts with various mass media. He keeps a table of those which appear to him most significant in adding a measure of breadth and depth to this knowledge. He asks which of the exposures further the objectives of a liberal and general education. He may label these objectives with such key phrases as "understanding the culture," "community concern," "building values," or "inspiration." His weekly tabulation form could look somewhat like this:

A WEEKLY RECORD OF EDUCATIONAL EXPERIENCES FROM PUBLIC COMMUNICATIONS						
Medium and place of encounter	Title of offering	Categories under which objectives fall				Resulting action
		Humanities	*Social Studies*	*Sciences*	*Health*	

One may begin an educational diary at any time of the year completely independent of an academic semester. The mass media are sufficiently rich in content to fill one's schedule with more liberal-general education than can be absorbed in countless lifetimes. Books are published about most topics at all levels of understanding. Magazines and newspapers appear regularly to inform, reinforce, and present choice and balance on topics about people, places and events. Recordings not only offer music but also can be used to enhance such areas as language, health, history, sociology and science. Great book classics are adapted into movies. Radio and television offer scheduled news reports and numerous occasions to witness history, science, technology, art and music in the making.

For the first few weeks of this self-education experiment, the learner need give no thought to his routine exposures to the mass media, which may include the paperback bookstand at a drugstore or supermarket, the magazine and newspaper rack in the airport terminal or at the hair dresser's, the radio in the car or on a boat, the television in the living room or lobby, the recorded selections heard on an elevator, and the matinee movie downtown after shopping. In any case, the educational offerings that are recorded will obviously be influenced by the kinds of interests he already holds. After a few weeks these interests will show a preponderant pattern on the chart, and the learner may turn to the challenge of filling in the gaps.

When he has become fully aware of the abundant education made possible largely by commercial ventures, he may add to the chart such professionally sponsored, non-classroom materials as may be encountered at the public library. At first he might randomly browse along the book or periodical shelves as he might have in the past, adding to his chart the increments of learning which become his own almost without effort. On a repeat visit, he will find himself using subject catalogues and indexes of the content of books, articles, recordings and television and radio programs. He will find these aids leading him to sources for additional clarification of his understanding of the goals, coverage and categories of a liberal and general education.

After about the seventh week, the learner is ready to fill in the column on the far right on his chart. This is the space for recording the action taken, the proof that he is knitting the various learnings together. He will ask himself such questions as these: In what further educational direction did the mass media experience send him? Did it lead to reflection, to a conversation, to a search in the encyclopedia, to a consultation with a scholar, to a visit to a laboratory or industrial firm, or to attendance at a lecture or concert? Did a program on radio or television, a book or magazine article, or a movie tie in directly with an experience via another medium in the same or in a preceding week?

The questions on relationships among educational experiences help to clarify objectives. The candidate for a liberal-general education will ask himself whether he is growing in an understanding of the cultural and scientific foundations, significant accomplishments, and unfinished business of his society. Is he building a set of values that will constitute a design for humane living? Does he feel a greater desire to appreciate the accumulated knowledge and honest opinion of other people, and to participate intelligently and responsibly in community life and public affairs? Do the leaders of stature in civic, political, economic, scientific, and cultural affairs seem less remote to him?

On answers to these questions the citizen bases his respect for education. The answers can stimulate parents pursuing a media self-education plan to engage in friendly competition with their children in school and thus make enjoyable the serious approach to formal course work. The venture will not directly bring an adult or youth the award of a diploma or degree, but it can certainly serve as a forceful instrument in that direction.

In varied forms, the media assignment is already being tried successfully on campus. The author has used it in the social sciences, humanities and education. For an American literature course, among the objectives he used was an awareness of the contemporary search for meaning in life. In political science teaching he dwelled upon principles of government, politics and citizen participation. For a course project in group behavior, he called on students to observe and analyze concepts of demoralization, persuasion, victimization, fad and fashion.

An English teacher joined forces with the media after noting the extensive vacation time which he and his students spent reading magazines and paperbacks, watching television and attending movies. He assigned television programs to be watched and popular magazine articles to be read; he used class time to discuss topics such as *cliche* and *generalization* and the transition of a story from book to television movie.[15] A profusely illustrated "worktext" developed to help realize the goals of a curriculum reform commission of the Journalism Education Association is based on the assumption that young people are profoundly influenced and, in fact, educated by the mass media. It aims to open the classroom walls and bring the media in to create a global classroom, a place where television, films, radio, newspapers, magazines and all types of advertising can be analyzed, understood and evaluated.[16] Defenders of the potential of "masspop" (electric environment created by mass media and popular culture) claim more effective teaching by going beyond appreciation to the stage of actually involving students in media-related activities, enabling its participants "to have a lot of good times and be entertained as well as educated."[17]

The widespread potential of this approach on campus dispels suspicions of campus separatism and smug independence from the public media. The citizen who has been puzzled about becoming educated finds the mysteries removed. Through his own eyes and ears, the media experiment has brought him the abundance of resources available to his fellow citizens, including those to whom he has entrusted the formal schooling of the nation's young people. He has structured the amorphous and unavoidable media influences on his life. Through his own effort, he has given them a meaning that harmonizes with the efforts of the academician and the curriculum builder. To anyone who considers it, the experiment highlights the truth that a person educated only in a classroom remains uneducated.

A MEDIA CURRICULUM

The chart described earlier indicates that the path to a liberal-general education involves a few relatively simple steps. The important question for the critical observer is: Who takes those simple steps? Research confirms the observation of many teachers that only the brightest students attempt it. Democracy clearly charges that this is not enough, that a citizenry is not ruled nor a culture sustained only, or even chiefly, by its self-motivated, best minds. More and more citizens must be helped to want to continue learning. They will not come to this without a new approach in the formal classroom.

The educator must realize that a school system has no magic or automatic formula by which to keep on a liberal path all who are by law or social pressure set upon it.[18] The educator must soon comprehend the full extent of his obligation—as a trusted and final arbiter on the content and objectives of all education and as a guide and mentor for anyone (especially the seeker and experimenter just described) who aspires to organize his mental growth toward meaningful ends. The educator is, in short, on the brink of facing the curriculum as an integrated combination of formal study with in-school and out-of-school mass media involvement. How can he accomplish this?

The instrument by which the schools seek to translate society's hopes for education into reality is the curriculum. It is the chief target of critics of teaching methods and course subjects. It is a pivotal concern of educators in their standardizing of teacher preparation and their promotion of better programs for students. In its original Latin, curriculum meant "a race track." For centuries, it was associated with schooling and learning, and the term now connotes something planned but not exactly final. Curriculum-making is a perennial task of review and revision of ideas and practices.

The concept of curriculum is not restricted to school experience. Decades ago, William Kilpatrick in his book, *Remaking the Curriculum*, stated that systematic learning must be founded on an ever-growing range of healthy interests and that "it is in the actual situations of life that learning best goes on."[19] Benson Snyder, a psychiatrist from MIT, used the term "invisible curriculum" to cover the informal failure, stress, and distress that are laid upon the student as an integral part of dynamic society.[20] Such varied daily experiences as domestic chores, personality conflicts, environmental pressures, taking a walk, or shopping for a used car can doubtless be educational, but they are not the overt teachers and teaching influences described in this book.

Curriculum in the schools is sometimes planned as a miniature process of living, with the total school experience portrayed as a replica of society. By joining student organizations and engaging in a variety of sponsored activities with classmates, a student does indeed enrich personality, share in a common culture, and learn to carry responsibilities with some similarity to the larger society. But the identification of a single social institution with the composite human society is narrow, confusing and contrived. The concept of the school as a "mini-society" is strained and may be abused by aggressive educators. A school may more effectively be thought of as a "midi-society," wherein school experiences are an intermediate step into broader social involvement.[21]

In the interest of exposure to society, courses frequently include field trips or visits to community establishments such as factories, banks, courtrooms and legislatures. But, as anyone who has been corralled from stop to stop during these trips knows, they can be as abstract and tedious as a poorly written textbook, and they are often characterized by the sparsity of deeper, lasting meanings. Similarly, schools and colleges arrange work-study programs in business and industry. Much more adaptable and useful educationally is that part of the total environment of living that constantly receives and reacts to modern mass media. In fact, awareness of a total life situation that shapes the mind of educated man is available through these extended eyes and ears. An apt name for a well-devised plan to pursue an education using media is a media curriculum.

The media approach respects the need for organization and relevance. About one of his characters, novelist Thomas Wolfe wrote: "He knew a great deal and understood almost nothing." Through the liberal-general education framework, a student can grasp vital relationships that lead to an understanding of the whole. If the media actually glut his communications intake with violence, habits of a dubious or unwanted nature, or sensationalism, he can immediately categorize them. He has no need for censorship; he passes judgment only on himself. In every instance, he places his learning in a meaningful context of human problems, needs, and aspirations—in short, he becomes his own best critic and censor.

Accompanying the drive and unrest of students is a demand for total involvement and rapid discovery of the whole picture. They seek "relevance," but segmented curricula and quantitative credit hours leave them wanting. At the beginning of formal education, a student rightfully calls for the ability to recognize a whole picture. As he proceeds, he asks for guidance in developing a meaningful plan for his life. Given an outline for seeking humane ends, a student is quite capable of developing the whole.

The "instructional materials" are largely what each student has seen and heard in his or her own everyday exposure to the media. So long as their public communicators continue to invade our lives, they are an inevitable, out-of-school influence on everyone. For anyone who is indecisive, they govern the daily schedule. Their impact can be positive or negative. On the one hand, the media are a vulgarization of and a threat to learning; on the other, they are a force for good and for inspiration. In either case, they are an irresistible attraction and behavior factor at all moments of everyday life, an ample illustration that "learning is caught as well as taught." Thus, it makes simple sense for the educational profession to make the mass media an area of serious curricular concern.

The new challenge from the mass media asks of the educator nothing impossible. Every teacher has the potential for using media offerings and adapting their techniques; he, too, is inescapably one of the members of the multimillion media audiences. More often than not, he has absorbed what is communicated because it has been so forcefully and repeatedly beamed at his most basic motivations, which are the very impulses he shares with his students and his fellow citizens. For use throughout the educational system, including in their own training, teachers urgently need handbooks of media logic, "grammars of the media," which will encourage universal education in the languages and values of the media by offering guidance in utilizing their content.

Educators are in a position to affect powerfully the mass media for the better. As in any progressive endeavor, they can see it not merely as it is, but also for its potential. They can encourage the publication of television and radio scripts. They can direct their students' and the public's attention to programs and films of permanent value. By entering into a new period of cooperation with the mass media, educational institutions can increasingly seek additional ways of testing and evaluating the non-classroom acquisition of learning so that its professional recognition will not be overlooked.

For many years, the representation of minority races on the mass media was rare. Television was in countless homes for two decades before any noticeable attention was given to presenting fairly the talent, the heritage, and the news of the Black population. An unfortunate and inaccurate stereotyping of minority races implanted false impressions and contributed to racism. In England, researchers reported that "the serpents of press and TV" had added "fuel for racial prejudice" by promoting material expectations and aspirations unobtainable to even the majority and, in doing so, engendered frustrations and unrest.[22] Similarly, in America, the media are said to have intensified racial conflict and alienation among some groups by picturing a society in which they had no part. Examining this criticism, the National Advisory Commission on Civil Disorders acknowledged incidents of inaccuracies, distortions, and sensationalism in the coverage of newspapers, radio, and television.[23]

Black communicators have fared better in recordings and on radio than in other media. At the same time, publishing has nurtured skillful writers of non-white races. Contemporary television features Black communicators in many ways. In fact, it was the help that came from the mass media, rather than the initiative from the schools, that was most effective in bringing about a gradual subsiding of racial unrest. Media people far more than educators helped to effect an integration whereby groups of different ethnic origin would engage in face-to-face communications.

The concept of a media curriculum coincides with the intensified efforts of schools, colleges, and universities to help correct media distortions and to examine their programs and staffing for more balanced representation of the heritage of minorities. Educators can continue the leadership in presenting a truer image of minority races and in helping individuals to use their talents as human beings. Liberal-general education comes alive as historians portray the struggle of the disadvantaged and the right to equal opportunities.

An appreciation of humanity accompanies liberal attitudes and general knowledge as a basic objective of education at all levels. The purpose of liberal education is to change people for the better. The formal curriculum has no reason for being other than to structure this purpose. It helps assure that the learner does grow in knowledge and wisdom, extend his interests in the welfare of others, and see life more fully. Classroom facts, figures, and experiences prescribed by educators constitute an identifiable and significant body of learning. The challenge lies in making it significant for everyone.

The building and pursuit of a curriculum are essentially the result of professional screening for what beyond the immediate present is worth knowing and expressing and believing. By contrast, mass media presentations are essentially a process of screening by society, collectively and individually, for knowledge and beliefs acceptable at present. A media curriculum integrates the disciplines of the professional educator with formal assignments and informal exposures from a full range of public mass media experiences. Far from being a nicely tied package of learning, unreal and isolated from life, a media curriculum is a continuing lifetime experience thoroughly implanted already at an early age. It could help to join together revolutions of education and the mass media. It could make possible a new educational philosophy that would cure educational schizophrenia.

8

A MASSIVE
CHALLENGE FOR
TOMORROW

Any worthwhile attempt to lift the curtain of the future presumes insight
and reflection, if not actual clairvoyance. Yet conjectures and projections
about education's future are rife. The ultimate revolution seems to be implied in the common forecasts that educational institutions as they exist
today will be changed almost beyond recognition by the year 2000. In the
preview and challenge for tomorrow's education and society, presented in
this chapter, no pretense is made to prophecy, but an inclination toward
laudable ideals is certainly intended.

In the sixteenth century writings of Thomas More, one identifies
with dauntless hopes of "a good place" where the educating and en-
nobling of all people banish ignorance, which is the cause of crime and
misery. Writing in the first part of the nineteenth century, Lewis Mumford indicated the importance of envisioning a reconstituted environment that is better adapted to the nature and aims of the human beings
who dwell within it. He regards it an absurdity to dispose of utopia by
saying that it exists only on paper.[1] Society today holds a reservoir of po-
tentialities, partly rooted in its past and partly budding forth from muta-
tions that open the way to ideal development. David Riesman defined
utopia as a rational belief in a potential reality, not violating human nature, yet transcending our present social organization.[2] This definition
befits the inspiring, yet simple words of Martin Luther King, Jr.: "I
have a dream."

In tomorrow's far better democracy, liberal-general education will
fulfill its objectives in relation to content and audience only in a plan that

thoroughly recognizes and uses the mass media. From this postulate flows a series of curricular and applied extensions and emphases. Training in basic skills and understandings will be directed with an eye toward clarified goals and meaningful organization in a setting expanded beyond the classroom. Recognizing the extreme brevity of an undergraduate student's association with persons in classrooms, libraries, and laboratories, educational statesmen have the grave responsibility of providing a curricular substance and plan that will stand in good stead for many years hence.

The public media will be appreciated and analyzed as a universal subject of study. They will be used and influenced through joint participation by learners and teachers. The device of criticism and the drive toward improvement will be constant and generally accepted companions. Self-reliance will have a new role in the pursuit of learning. The true function of the college will come into sharper focus. The teacher will grow in influence and prestige. Education will become a normal part of everyone's life. All this will come about as the reader analyzes these propositions and adapts and enlarges upon them as his very own challenge.

BASIC SKILLS AND UNDERSTANDINGS

Effective human relations in modern society demand the greatest clarity of individual expression and understanding. The curricular panacea for the 1970s emphasizes the understanding of self and the resolving of identity conflicts and crises. The school will continue to provide experiences and guidance in value choices that are developmental and positive for students. It is basic that the child emerge through adolescence into adulthood convinced of his or her ability to influence the formulation of a social environment that will help further to actualize human potential. It cannot be overemphasized that the success of today's many, laudable programs is interwoven with the revolutionary changes in technology and population patterns, which can be either a threat or a hope for future human life. The direction will depend upon the capacity of human beings to communicate with at least a minimum of human understanding.

Communications skills are already represented in a core of courses on presenting and perceiving spoken, heard, read and written intercourse. For the most part, these courses are little more than adaptations or expansions of the traditional textbook approach in English rhetoric and composition. Some curricula have combined skills in at least one language other than English and in mathematics. These courses carry out the basic task of providing citizens with the means of personal communications for daily living. This is the part of education that the schools can and will continue to do best. In doing so, they will increasingly make use of the mass media both for content and method.

At the higher levels of education, course offerings are more diverse. There are the compartmentalized facts and figures, ideas and viewpoints, of the humanities, social studies, natural and physical sciences, and health and physical education. Although they are well established in academic institutions, these traditional subject groupings and the specific subjects within each do not in themselves contribute to the best means of meeting liberal and humanitarian objectives. Indeed, the broader objectives and needs wage a running battle with departmental and divisional sectarianism, a cancerous condition wherein the promoters of a given area of learning attempt to ignore the importance of other areas. The very terms "liberal arts" or "general studies," listed in a college catalogue opposite terms such as "applied arts" or "specialized studies," must be repeatedly clarified. As humane studies, they cannot and should not survive exclusively as if they were cataclysmically different, as if one area had no bearing on another.

Conducted by a farsighted disciplinarian, a traditional study *does lead* to liberal-general education, informed judgment, sound reasoning and the ability to transfer learning from one subject to another. Charles Frankel eloquently describes the studies as liberal if they lift the student from the domination of what is conventional and near at hand, if they pierce the veil of the commonplace.[3] However, it takes a personal determination to survey the dimensions of the garden and the wealth of varieties it can generate to bring out a vigorous growth that enables one to reap an abundant harvest.

The media scholar, Wilbur Schramm, states that people emerge from school with "a cognitive map, an organized life space, and certain skills and habits." Continuing education, he said, means "more reading skill and a better-filled-in map, which in turn means wider interests and a greater appetite for information."[4]

Controversial debate of critical issues is a long-standing feature of university and college life. The values of conflicting opinion for its own sake are often extolled, and a campus often appears to be a dynamo of new and radical ideals. Knowledge seems to rise from intellectual challenge and ferment. Like many other relationships, however, such as the behavioral effect of certain media content, the benefits of debate solely for its own sake cannot be proved or disproved. They have, in fact, become highly suspect by many. The liberal arts and general studies, while resulting in discussion, include disciplined coordination of knowledge and ideas with the aim of developing a measure of harmony among the participants. When it is free of menial fractionalization, the campus is a greenhouse for new and valid ideas and a stimulus to variety, and most of all, it is a resource for human direction. Mass media should share in this role.

The professing of a right direction will always be an avowed purpose of education. In a church-related institution, the integration of mind, body, and spirit is self-evident. Other institutions, however, also seek the positive goal of a whole person, including his or her spiritual involvement. Church-sponsored chapels and facilities are located near the campus. In a call-to-action statement by the Regents of the University of the State of New York, schools and colleges are required to foster conviction with respect to moral and spiritual values and to develop habits of self-discipline and regard for the rights of others as "rooted in an abiding knowledge and practice of one's obligations to God our Creator, and to man, our brother."[5] At the same time, they must prepare people to live in a scientific-technological society, develop an understanding of other peoples as an essential element in cooperation for peace, and maintain the American spirit of meeting new conditions with resourcefulness and self-assurance. It bears repeating that nothing in the list suggests cultivation of controversy or derisiveness as an avenue to understanding.

Speaking to all media, the radio commentator John Daly stated his concern with the ethics, standards, principles, taste, objectivity, editorial honesty, and conviction of media people.[6] He raised the question of whether these basic qualities have faltered under the torrents of confusion and conflicts in the age of atoms and space. He suspected that they have. Using illustrations ranging from assassinations and court rulings to religion and war, he spelled out the need for more truthful reporting and editorial selectivity concerning public affairs. There can be no doubt that far more important than greater speed and coverage in communications is the manner in which the focus is on truth and uplift.

In the interest of humanization, foundations and government agencies have poured millions of dollars into academic institutions while also aiding the communications industries. The support comes not only because of a positive interest in the validity of increasing people's understandings and skills but also, as an annual report of the Carnegie foundation stated, because the undergraduate liberal education that nurtures them is on trial for its life and is not to be saved by pious appeals or on the grounds of tradition.[7] Unfortunately, the approach of many foundations and agencies, as well as of campus administrations, has been largely defensive, and the emphasis on whatever specialized subject areas are in vogue has taken precedence over more general programs.

THE EXPANDED SETTING

Traditionally, the classroom has been the focus for teaching the basic skills and subject matter that add to general knowledge and foster liberal understandings. The classroom will continue to be the mainstream, supplemented by such electronic laboratories and automated instructional centers as will eventually prove acceptable in releasing teachers for more individual attention to students. Together with multifarious architectural innovations, these technical changes may be described as revolutionary. But the really revolutionary change in setting and technique for higher education will come when the campus reaches out to the mass media of public communication and intimately ties both to the broader content of a general-liberal education. Closely allied to lecture, discussion, textbooks, and programs for the classroom will be the best that the media can offer for every citizen. The skills of expression and reporting, together with the content of the humanities, social studies, and sciences, as available directly or indirectly through radio, television, recordings, film, books, newspapers, and magazines, will be presented in convenient form. In the carefully planned class agenda, all these resources are necessary to a comprehensive climate of learning, without which the effort of college may be wasted.

Professional organizations will work with mass media operators and sponsors to assist a curriculum committee in coordinating free educational content on the mass media. Committee members will be able to monitor radio and television program offerings up until the last moment before a pertinent class meeting or an extracurricular event. Administration, faculty members, and students will realize the value of incorporating these in assignments. A recurring question will be whether or not an available mass media offering might not best fulfill a particular objective of the course.

A professor's reference to a late news event, to headlines in the paper, or to a significant television or radio program just aired or soon to be aired will be commonplace. It will often be desirable to precede a classroom program with a five-minute overview of the headlined articles and editorial page of the morning newspaper, a media news analysis, an international conference, or a concert commentary. The instructional tie with the contemporary and the co-incident will be intimate.

At any hour of the school day, a class may use special radio or television reports, cultural programs, and news summaries. Students also will be expected to hear and view programs that are scheduled during out-of-school hours. These will be regular assignments, along with reading in newspapers, periodicals, and paperbacks; attendance at movies; and listening to recordings. They will have a place not only in English and social studies, where the pioneering has taken place,[8] but also throughout the curriculum in imaginative ways fostered by professional periodicals on this new style of teaching.

The assignment of a term project will direct the student to observe what the mass media add to his knowledge and understanding of the selected topic. Class reports on the resulting insights gleaned from the media will be as generally accepted as the conventional reports on reading library books. At election times, report writing, class discussion, or textbook reading will be expanded through initial and simultaneous use of obvious sources such as articles and cartoons in newspapers and magazines; news commentaries and political announcements; campaign speeches; and interviews on recording, radio, and television. Students may be given individual and group responsibilities to collect all available information on various candidates, policies, issues, and opinion polls. They will welcome an opportunity to assemble, organize, and report on the contemporary scene of which they are already aware.

At once, the learning-teaching process will be both simplified and enriched. For the learner, the approach will be both convenient and attractive. Computers will be prominent study aids, supplying students specific information, rather than inundating them with an avalanche of data they do not want or cannot use.

In a real sense, the student will be undergoing a learning process toward freedom. The elements of learning previously discussed—transfer, imitation, repetition, and motivation—will converge with self-paced learning. Media curricula that draw on the vast non-classroom milieu will motivate the student to seize the challenge of transferring and broadening his learning. They will help to bring order out of the bafflement and chaos caused by the indiscriminate oversupply of data, at the same time facilitating the development of initiative and responsibility. Motivation will be founded on personal values. Learning will become free of rigidity and unnatural constrictions.

Students in all classes will keep notebook records of their actual and potential mass media learnings in each subject and will develop this kind of exercise as a lasting habit. From time to time the teacher will distribute a schedule, a new kind of bibliography, for the subject he teaches to make certain that no important media offerings are overlooked. No student or citizen will ever again have occasion to doubt that education is plentiful in a world of mass media.

Research on the effectiveness of the mass media will parallel research on the effectiveness of the classroom. A single medium or a single teaching-learning situation will continue to intrigue scholars and researchers, but they will also proceed to the broader perspective of interrelationships among all of the media, commercial and noncommercial, and between classroom theory and communications practice. Publishers, broadcasters and film producers will benefit from the research as they prepare new combinations of printed matter, film and recordings to supplement television and radio programs. They will enjoy cooperation with academic institutions in enriching and meeting the common objectives of a democratic society. The two cultural forces of schooling and the media, which the author has described in an article in *College and University*, will be widely used for becoming educated.[9]

Any citizen will be able to obtain a schedule of educational offerings and many will keep personal notebooks similar to those of students who are completing assignments for specific courses. Their purpose will be to increase their sense of awareness and to clarify and enhance their self-education. A personal plan of education may bring into its orbit such leisure activities as playing cards, collecting salt shakers, hiking, camping, bowling, fiddle-playing, or watching baseball, but hardly with time-killing as an objective. More citizens will see leisure as an essential to wisdom, an activity that can be kindled by learning and teaching.

A Vital Course for Everyone

The awareness and use of an expanded setting for education will lead to the addition of a new curricular subject taught on a wide scale: the study and appreciation and the languages and values of public communications. It may well become the most essential course of study in democracy's curriculum for tomorrow, as fundamental as English or mathematics, for every citizen is actually or potentially a mass media recipient. In that great audience, one can be either master or servant, depending in large measure upon the perception of the operations involved.

The steps to understanding the mass media can be very elaborate and intricate, or they can be relatively simple. The National Association of Educational Broadcasters, in cooperation with the United States Office of Education, for example, some time ago proposed the development of "grammars of the media" for the use of teachers and students.[10] Several of the works listed in the bibliographical notes of this book are helpful in this vein. Future textbooks will become even more effective aids for receiving mass-communicated information, opinion, and fiction. In the words of the preface writer of the book *Media for the Millions*, new manuals and guides will help communications to be received "with neither gullability nor rejection but with objective and critical discrimination."[11]

The outline for the course on the mass media for everyone will likely include (a) historical development and parallels among the media, (b) technical devices, the styles, and the methods, (c) the economic foundations and institutional setting, and (d) the psychological and sociological role of the media and the human needs they meet. With due regard for flexibility, the approach to understanding can be thought of as an examination of the structure and process of a social institution. The course will go beyond what have been called "pipsqueak communication theories" of academicians or "smug assumptions" of media leaders.[12]

Through the classroom, the student will have learned to benefit from the varied mass media offerings and to see himself as a member of an audience in search of specific content. Public communications will become an enlargement and expansion of the school. The student will realize the relationship of his own part to the whole communications process and the necessity for constantly seeking the improvement of all of its elements. By learning the arts of criticism and coordination, of evaluation analysis and synthesis, he will become what one writer has coined, a "critical receiver."[13] He need never hesitate about encountering media producers on his own. In addition he will have reenforced the value of self-reliance.

A notable example of planning for a media curriculum has occurred in Australia under the aegis of parochial schools and with the blessing of the Australian Broadcasting Commission. Acknowledging the impact of the public media, the plan is one of curricular guidelines for the schools. From a bishop's conference came the comment: "It is necessary for all to learn how to control these marvels of human intervention and not let them control us."[14] Without deprecating any part of the regular curriculum, the planners state that, in a changing situation, schools must teach students to distinguish good from bad in radio, television, and press.

A civic-minded leader, scholar, or teacher will continue to study technical know-how in communications and all possible uses of mechanical and electronic automation, but his chief concern will increasingly be an awareness of humanity that will give framework to learning. Aimless infatuation with the forms and mechanics of communicating and teaching will be nonexistent. "No matter how skillful man becomes in analyzing and controlling the methods and techniques of communication," writes a psychiatrist, "we will still be faced with the problems of meaning and value, of which content is more desirable, more valuable, more favorable to use at any stated time."[15]

ANALYSIS AND SYNTHESIS

Modern public communications envelop every student and citizen in a constant condition of learning. Newspapers, magazines, books, radio, movies, television, and recordings dominate even the learning he receives through directly observing and imitating his parents, teachers, and other associates. As people mature, the media increasingly take over their lives, either by extending their experience, wisdom, and vision or by narrowing their insight and making them indifferent dilettantes or apathetic fools. The media may also leave one's mind perpetually disorganized, as James Russell Lowell's poem, "Fable for Critics," so cleverly describes:

'Twould be endless to tell you the things that he knew
Each a separate fact, undeniably true.
But with him or each other they'd nothing to do;

No power of combining, arranging, discerning
Digested the masses he learned into learning.[16]

From any liberal-general curriculum, a student can be presumed to absorb only a small fraction of the data of science, the details of literature, or the events and names of people in history and government. Similarly, the facts, ideas, and figures relayed by the mass media are too copious to grasp. How ridiculous to suggest that anyone could or should attempt to read, see, or hear all that is made public. As obvious as this statement seems, many people fail to see the necessity for discriminating selection and coordination of mass media activities. Yet sensitive viewer reaction can be responsible for the prevention of investigatory orgies by government that are fanned and prolonged by the mass media for audience effect.

The enormous confusion of modern communications has progressively made new and frightening demands on the individual. More than at any other time in history, he is forced to make complicated choices having both immediate and ultimate purposes. Intelligent selectivity becomes a basic function for anyone who would be more than a sieve or a sponge. A crude but telling analogy may be made to other basic human activities. Few persons would deliberately allow low quality food on their tables, dirty rags to clothe their bodies, or a botch of sticks and stones to pass for a house. Anyone would consider it grotesque to wallow among mounds of everybody's food, clothing, and shelter. A picture of masses of individuals, purposeless and gullible, rolling about in a mire of mass media effusion ought to be equally ludicrous.

Just as people learn to exercise intelligent choice in their daily purchases, they should and will learn to discriminate between the wholesome and unwholesome, helpful and harmful, efficient and inefficient offerings of the mass media. They will avoid passivity. The new media approach to learning will instill the excitement of education beyond the classroom. The fruits of liberal education will prevent them from joining either the media extreme that yells "Down with Everything!" or its counterpart, which yields to the temptation to get on all of the bandwagons. Citizens will see the need to identify a meaningful and orderly pattern in their own lives and to understand its inconsistencies.

To meet the modern challenge, people must habitually seek truth and right action. The mass media outpourings have already given people practice, for few other life experiences incite the public so frequently to criticism. More important, the art of constructive comment, of giving sincere compliments and votes of confidence, is vital in a healthy society. To paraphrase one educator's words about curriculum in the public schools, higher education exists primarily to foster constructive criticism of our institutional life and to cultivate an intelligent citizenship to act accordingly. Limiting "such study and criticism as to possible desirable changes," he adds, is "exactly an effort to foster social blindness and stupidity."[17]

Along with the acquisition of basic skills, the student will adopt the critical equipment necessary to focus and express his impartial dissatisfaction and thoughtful discernment with the media. Through a media curriculum, he will have learned to put himself beyond the influence of extravagant display, cheap publicity, big-name advertisers, and clever conspiracy. He will learn to judge dramatic content on its own merits. Just as the school has for many decades counseled young people on reading and appreciation of drama, music, and art, it will, in the future, also counsel everyone in the cultivation of good taste in radio, television, recordings, and movies. Citizens will engage in what a UNESCO spokesman calls "campaigns of critical appraisal."[18] They will examine the facts and clarify their values before they judge media content, and they will convey effectively their suggestions for its improvement.

Whatever role a person fills, he will make use of rather specific actions to suit his particular needs, moods, and obligations. Stanley Hyman, a journalist and critic, as well as parent and teacher, has compiled a list which is very provocative here. It is a list of what he calls operative verbs, which are paraphrased as follows: *Reject.* The slogan to aim at Hollywood and television might be: "destroy their destructiveness." Expose the pernicious trash in every way possible. *Embrace.* Welcome wholeheartedly the superior paperback. *Ignore.* Let students keep private any tyrannous underground circular which speaks to their condition. *Improve.* Exercise the pedagogic tactic of using what the student likes as a guidepost to something better. *Replace.* Bring to the attention of the learner the greatest of literature, the best that has been thought and known. *Warn.* In a good, stout voice, bellow and curse and call down doom, like the prophet Jeremiah.[19]

The objective is not to build an adjusted personality, although this may result. It is rather to give citizens the examples of excellence that will let them take a fresh look at the world around them, feel uncomfortable with mediocrity, and rebel against vulgarity and stupidity. It is to remove the priggishness or disdain that accompanies ignorance of good things not adequately or necessarily labeled educational. The spirit of critical analysis is part of the act of shaping experience into rational and human terms communicable to others. According to a conference resolution of the American Association for Higher Education, a unique college and university role is that of advancing society "by serving as its critic, helping it envision what it can become, and measuring the extent of its progress toward that goal."[20]

Wedged between the two revolutions of mass media and higher education, the educator is caught up in a centrifuge of knowledge. Infinite breadth and depth vie with each other in his mind and challenge him to wisdom. Breadth and depth of figures and other information in endless array vie, in turn, with the knowledge of purpose, values, goals and con-sequences—what the philosophers call teleology. The educational task will be to bridge both the knowing and the purposeful, to screen out bar-riers that are obstructions to human progress.

The role of colleges and universities will be to guide the transition from chaos to that discernment that leads to orderliness and creativity. It will blend the fullness of the freedom to read and see and hear with an awareness of the need for selecting what is best. The challenge to a lib-eral-general educator will be to bind with a common denominator the many separate, often combative numerators of mass media disunion. Stu-dents and scholars on campuses will share an identity of purpose and, as Harold Taylor affirms in a book on social change, an induction into the actual problems and promises of the social order and of the human race.[21]

SELF-RELIANCE

It is not stretching the possibilities of the future to assert that the worldwide "classrooms" of the mass media will cut the students' pedago-gical apron strings and give them a new perspective on management of the learning process. Education by means of credit hours and class schedules in high school and the first two college years is largely an ar-rangement of spoon-feeding. The student comes to class and says, in ef-fect, "Here I am; teach me, feed me." He gives back in examination and recitation the lapped-up rations that the teacher has assigned as "home-work." The relationship, alternatively, is like a contract in that it termi-nates with the receipt of a letter grade or a diploma.

The removal of specifically prescribed "divisions," "periods," and "amounts" of learning is unnecessary. Moreover, it is impossible. Cen-sure or grievance is misdirected when it ignores what the schools are and can honestly claim to be. Organized periods and stages of learning are merely a convenient way of embarking on the formal adventure of seri-ous learning. The award of a degree for completion of the steps is not a proof of learning; it is a formality in recognition of such academic steps as examination, attendance, recitation, and official record-keeping. The stu-dent, employer, or civic leader who accepts these as anything more de-serves to be disappointed.

Campus instruction will no longer leave a student restricted to class assignment after assignment and conditioned response after response. Moreover, school will never appear, even to a rebel, as a network of indi-vidual and institutional whims and fancies of personality and curriculum. Students will not, in the future, traverse the required school years only to find, upon completion, that theirs was not real education. The four years will, indeed, have been genuine, because they will have stressed that learning is the enterprise of a lifetime. The proof of having become educated, they will know, comes outside and after the classroom and is quite apart from a diploma.

Schooling that repeatedly emphasizes education begun and fostered informally can make of the student an honest seeker of knowledge and a happy devotee of learning. Along with the incentives of credit hours and a diploma, this emphasis has already been offered to exceptional students, who are often given the privilege of unassigned reading and reporting or of participation in honors programs and seminars. In a mass-media society, the school must, however, offer incentives for everyone who desires to learn continuously; this is the educator's solemn and least-understood obligation.

In facing and studying the heavy outpouring of all the media, in sorting out alternatives and clarifying goals, the learner will have undergone imaginative and creative steps. He will have visualized experiences charted under the major categories of an academic curriculum and its objectives. From here, he can put his own "curriculum" into operation, watching to see how it works, looking back to see what was done, and anticipating how it might be more effective. He can lay out a comprehensive life plan of personal intellectual growth to be nourished by the mass media.

Thus, while training the individual in the personal skills of communication and orienting him in the breadth of human knowledge, the campus will guide him toward proper resources. In his course work, he will take steps not unlike those of the seasoned scholar. As he becomes aware of the abundant knowledge that is freely disseminated, he will experience the rewarding hard work of using it in research that has direction. He will come to know that his education is meaningful because it is self-guided.

Every citizen who wants to assume a large measure of individual responsibility will receive the training to do so. He will no longer be inclined to point to schools or the media or the family or the government, or any institution or individual as a scapegoat. Paul Dressel of Michigan State University stated that a college education is successful if it leads to responsibility for self-education; it is a waste if it fails in this. On the television show, "Meet the Professor," Joseph deFrance noted: "The student learns only when he takes an active part in the teaching-learning process."[22] In charting the course of the college, Freeman Butts affirmed that the best learning "encourages the learner himself to take the initiative in planning, carrying out, and judging his own activities" and that the test of learning is "the ability to act intelligently in subsequent experiences."[23]

In brief, learning in a formal, certified manner is not a prerequisite to meeting the objectives of a true education. The incentives of the credit hour and the diploma are of only secondary concern. All students, gifted and nongifted, will one day realize that real education comes through free effort outside the school and campus walls. They are closer to a liberal-general education when they have their own experiences than when they merely study those of others. To paraphrase a writer on the plight and possibility of liberal education, they themselves must "hear the music."[24] The proper and indispensable role of the campus is to offer guidance for formal and out-of-school education, with a professional and informed teacher acting as a consultant not as a dictator. In this role, educators can also bring the vital interpersonal contact that the public media lack.

A PARTNERSHIP FOR EDUCATION

It is folly to expect that the desire, pursuit, and admiration of education will ever be as natural as the need to eat or to sleep. It may be unlikely that education for large numbers of persons will become as essential as religion, although the two are intertwined. But it is entirely probable that education can be among the normal, conscious activities of everyone. It is entirely appropriate that the dedicated teacher should be as admired and familiar a public acquaintance as the star fullback, comedian, cartoonist, crooner, politician, or evangelist has become in our society. Would any friend of education deign to discourage this advancement?

The barriers that make the pursuit of education a lonesome one will tumble. Teachers will no longer be split personalities: teacher by day and spectator by night. They will see their daytime professional endeavors take on the best qualities of show business and Madison Avenue. More than ever, teachers will apply their talents directly to humanizing, enlivening, and personalizing their knowledge for greater teaching effectiveness. The educator and his team will be the new star with something to say.[25]

The teacher-communicator will be duly rewarded. High salaries for educators will be commonplace. Morris Ernst in his book, *Utopia 1976*, may have missed the mark somewhat when he stated that "the principal of a school will earn more than the head of a funeral parlor and a college professor may be paid as much as a left fielder."[26] Still, as the economic status of teachers does grow, the reason will not lie in their bargaining power or in their internal pressures on administrators and trustees, but rather, in their services to the eager public they have impressed. The reason will not lie in campus recruitment literature that misinterprets education as a path to careers of more money and less drudgery, but in the widely recognized change of emphasis from the getting of lessons to the. getting of wisdom, from the love of money to the love of learning and teaching. Knowledge and wisdom will not be desecrated at the level of a mere commodity sold by teachers who are then evaluated as salesmen by students forced into the awkward role of purchasers.

Formal testing of the memorization and reproduction of facts and figures will decrease. The cat-and-mouse games of examinations and grades between teacher and student will be superseded by the love of learning and the respect for teaching. The measuring of intelligence and achievement will be used more appropriately to free the student to take advantage of testing as an aid to learning. Neither frightened, shamed, nor otherwise pressured into completing assignments, the student will find learning natural. Mass-media learning will be recognized for credit.

With the conviction that the campus is the center of enlightenment, the educator will continue to develop the procedures and facilities to aid the groping mind on its way toward excellence. To everyone, it will remain clear that the campus must provide the laboratories, shops, studios, classrooms, libraries, and exhibits necessary to intensive formal study and experimentation, but in all cases, their formal use will readily adapt to the less-formal, day-to-day application in human affairs. Given the springboard of the whole media force of teaching awareness and effectiveness, students will utilize campus facilities with revived vigor and enthusiasm.

The multiversity concept that diffuses knowledge and confuses learners will refocus as a university concept to unify knowledge and integrate learners. The falsity in making specialization a dogma of departmentalized limitations will be exposed. Educators will be released from the imprisonment of a single highly disciplined specialty. Implicit in an appointment to teach in a program of liberal arts or general studies will be the expectation that liberality, breadth, and humanity will be deeply ingrained and voluntarily maintained. Cross-disciplinary activity among faculty members will become normal. They will be encouraged to show genuine interest and ability beyond the narrow confines of a single field. Every professor will have the opportunity to deliver lectures and lead discussions on topics not directly related to his own specialty. Indeed, each will be a specialist in more than one area.

A long-standing complaint is that commercial sponsorship of broadcasts, publications, films, and recordings is a serious obstacle to advancing educational and cultural endeavors. Offerings of high caliber are lost to millions or never made public at all because they are not commercially sponsored, promoted, or owned. Defenders of a Marxist system of government ownership of the press ask how capitalists can have any honest interest in education if it doesn't pay off in dollars. Admirers of British or French television and radio lament that the United States as the only great nation that allows the best audience hours of the day to be used by private agencies seeking to sell things to the public. On the American mass media, critics say, culture is given as a favor, chiefly for the commercial goodwill expected in return; it is window dressing.[27] In the future, the two million people who take Sunrise Semester courses at dawn will become many more millions taking courses at noon or at sunset, and receiving other educational values during prime time.

The arts are fundamental in communication and their frequently varied patrons will increasingly become one. As Thomas Guback pleads in an article in *The Journal of Aesthetic Education*, a journalistic and sociopsychological bias flows from a general lack of concern for the arts and their role as a mode of socialization. It is necessary, he emphasizes, that courses about mass communication, therefore, must not only examine media content as a surface phenomenon, but also study its sources and how decisions about content are made. This means a close scrutiny of the social context of communication. It means that, as the world expands spatially and intellectually, the confrontation is increasingly through the agencies of communication."[28]

Confronted with a paradox between values and masses, the teacher and the communicator together will lead in setting the issues straight. The creation and dissemination of cultural values have for centuries had sponsors: the government, the nobility, or the church. Symphonies, paintings, and sculpture have been commissioned by royalty or patronized by aristocracy. Sponsorship, then as now, is necessary, and its critical questions relate to the unfair exploitation of talent and the breeding of public gullibility. To these, the educator and the communicator will jointly bring answers through the revitalized liberal-general curriculum.

The communicator has been attuned to mass audiences, to reaching for the average or common denominator in people, even while using the appeal and taste of those more refined. The educator, skilled in working face-to-face with individuals, will help to humanize the media. Like those individuals in some classrooms with antiquated methodology, the members of an audience of public communications should be no faceless blobs, but human personalities potentially as different as their fingerprints. It is possible that, with educator influence, the term "mass" will need replacement.

It is sensitivity to the individual recipient of the learning or other communication that will count most. In Shaw's *Pygmalion*, Eliza explains: "The difference between a lady and a flower girl is not how she behaves, but how she's treated. . . . I know I can be a lady to you because you always treat me as a lady, and always will."[29] The success of the communicator, at least in part, will be due to his having high and positive expectations of the members of his audience; the hope and demand of professors for enthusiastic responses from students will no longer be considered slight. The mass communicator of the future will come to laud the teacher as one who seeks only high values and top performance.

Just as in good pedagogy, an instructor begins at the intellectual and informational level of most of the class, so also the broadcaster or publisher begins at the level common to the greatest audience. The most effective message fits the pattern of understandings, values, and goals of the receiver. It is no cause for alarm, one critic stated, if surveys show that the public's first choices are comedy, rock, sports, Westerns, or whatever. It is more practical to note that second choices are drama, news analyses, personality interviews, classics, or homemaking—all with clear educational potential. Although the ideal media content might be something similar to a philosophical voyage or scholarly disquisition, "the human situation," as W. Macneile Dixon wrote, requires a beginning and sometimes a remaining with the familiar world of commonly held values, the joys and sorrows of everyday existence.[30]

Whatever the choices, the educator at least now will know the platform on which one can raise tastes. He will see the launching pad that commercial interests have built; he will want to influence the orbits they choose to make. He will let the sponsors know that his curriculum uses their offerings and that the student has learned to approach them discriminatingly, to use them wisely, and to seek their improvement. He will be pleased to have his professional offerings, whether they be classroom sessions, special convocations, or discussion programs, underwritten by the commercial sponsors.

The teacher will program ideas and scripts for television and radio, and write editorials and articles for mass magazines and newspapers. Learning exercises, including crossword puzzles and quiz columns, will be as widely followed as the comics or the sports page. Professorial lectures will appear in newspapers throughout the country, not only in scattered locations about which *Time* magazine reported in an article "College by Newspaper."[31] A television or radio program aimed at critical problems will be such that young people will want to attend to it. Whatever the significant topic, it will elicit the same approval as a *Saturday Review* critic gave to "VD Blues," an event that brings enlightenment and raises consciousness, rather than being "a medium for mind-rotting schlock."[32] An educator will be engaged to lend his talents and those of his students to these programs, as well as to commercial films and recordings. He will frequently be an author capable of meeting mass media deadlines and other requirements. The teacher will write and speak in order to be understood by the citizenry. He will add spirit and drama to his subject presentation and without losing respectability, he will exercise showmanship.

Instead of avoiding the professional teacher, the commercial media will welcome and even seek him out. Sponsors will encourage him to place added stress on originality, dynamism, and enthusiasm. They will give to the teacher the widest horizon of content and help him build a larger audience than he has ever dreamed possible. Mass media sponsors will expand their efforts to provide supplementary aids for the classroom, making them available also to members of the great audience outside the schools. The media that reach audiences numbering in the millions will take the lead in encouraging dissemination of educational content by other channels reaching large numbers, whether such channels be cereal cartons at the breakfast table, commemorative postage stamps, billboards, or direct mail.

The media sponsors will insist that their commercial messages be presented with good taste and prudence, since profits and education will not be in conflict. The do-or-die race for top television ratings and the cutthroat battles for press coverage will dwindle away. The industrialist and businessman will strive to improve the humanitarian quality of their products and services. They will also increase their monetary donations and tax support to education. Media self-regulation will be fully effective, and the role of government will be minimal. In turn, the educator will understand the need for fair profit and give frequent recognition to the commercial media, their sponsors, and advertisers. "Oscars," "Emmys" and other media awards for distinguished performance will be supplemented by awards for educational service. The campus administrator, faculty member, and student will exhibit as much pride and pleasure in lauding the achievements of the mass media as they do now in acknowledging donations of money or buildings or in granting academic degrees and other honors.

The intellectual and economic seduction and exploitation of the teacher as a textbook writer, for example, and the betrayal of the public that once characterized a quiz show, will no longer be possible, because the commercial supporters will place a higher premium on human values than on sales records. The teacher will not prostitute his professional dignity and personal integrity by remaining in the shadows. He will place full value on honest education and unpretentious scholarship and will abhor being the submissive instrument of any community power-elite.

If harsh brutalities, cynicism, or deceit enter the mass media, the educator will explain them and set them right. If the mass media show the world changing so rapidly as to place historical precedent out of focus, the educator will restore the perspective. If the public communications climate appears to be exclusively for pleasure-seekers and irresponsible persons, it will be corrected with the substance of learning and teaching. If skepticism is being ploughed into the furrows of a young mind, the educators will restore and justify a faith in authority. There will be no room for pontification by faculty or suspicions by students, no assumptions that professors only lead and teach and students only follow and learn, which one writer notes as likely problems in curriculum reform.[33]

Together both teacher and student, as well as the great public, will be less susceptible to the bribe that mediocrity often uses as its only weapon. Instead of knowing the schools as a chief refuge for those interested in music, art, literature, and other human endeavors, the classroom student will locate or demand the finest talents of the mass media. Educators will vigorously promote a balance between social responsibility and creative endeavor, individual freedom and individual restraint. The student will respond with a strong program of action. A positive answer will be given to the question raised by author Joseph Wood Krutch: "Can we have an Age of the Common Man without making it an Age of the Common Denominator?"[34]

An Education-Centered Community

The example and the training in mass media understanding and participation on the part of educators will have a widespread influence on the public. It will carry specific suggestions for bringing all of the media into the service of democracy. The educator will have succeeded in cultivating the highest human taste and value among mass media offerings. The climate of learning will be transformed, filtering through all levels. The public will be making itself an alert, discriminating audience, which William Rivers and Wilbur Schramm describe as its first responsibility.[35] All citizens not able or eager to attend classes will enjoy an abundance of education as a window on the world and an expansion of horizons.

The noble goal—the attainment of a "learning society"—will be met as much through the media as through the classroom. The expectation of doing so by exclusive concentration on increasing the scope and power of formal education is already coming to a halt. Formal enrollment will not be the educational issue of the future any more than it should be in the present. The goal of a new community will be reached when individuals are empowered to learn and grow by using the resources, community support, and self-motivation to move forward on their own. What is predicted as a nation of learners will enjoy opportunities to learn in abundant measure throughout society and throughout the span of life.[36]

The partnership of learning and teaching will be a concept known to everyone in the new generation. With the privilege of the former will come a responsibility for the latter. If a student's vocational choice is to participate in the formal education of others, he or she will be able immediately and clearly to transfer the spirit of learning to the excitement of teaching.

Regardless of vocational ambition, the new dimensions of a media curriculum will motivate every student to teach and to practice what he has learned. He will understand the role of the mass media as highly powerful inculcators of information and stimulators of action. Working under dedicated teachers who will encourage him to understand the overview of historical and contemporary experience, he will be caught by the sense of urgency to participate. He will know that much more remains to be done. Like every responsible citizen, the alumnus will regard the mass media as something of a second alma mater from which he can continue to take much learning and to which he is obliged to return more. He will happily act to influence public communications toward increasingly rational and humane social purposes.

The mass media will always be dependent upon regular audiences for their existence. Their operators will always be sensitive to the opinions and behaviors of the great public. In the knowledge that a cultural clientele will demand good viewing, listening, and reading of all kinds, the sponsors will change their offerings. Through education, the public will have sounder opinions. The Federal Trade Commission will no longer need to censure deceptive advertising. A wiser public will ignore exaggerations, disparagement, inane logic, and saturation-campaign excesses. Moreover, further revolutionary technology will help make such practices obsolete.

Writing letters in order to swell the deluge of influence from a pressure group or vested interest, or taking an audience role in paid applause, prearranged laughter, or manufactured tears will gradually cease. Letters and other responses to a performance or publication will express honest, individual views and reflect the wisdom obtained from a liberal-general education. At times, the exercise of this privilege in a democracy will be as important an obligation as going to the polls on election day. In turn, the effect of the exercise of this privilege on the course of community affairs will often be just as significant as voting.

Relationships with governmental units will be similar for both the schools and the mass media. National interests in education and communications will be considered through a new cabinet-level department, promoting local projects to inform, enlighten, entertain, and help all of the citizenry and to set for them the highest of humanitarian ideals. With far more education available than was ever dreamed possible through classrooms alone, offices for health and welfare will adopt new concepts of service. More individuals will be better able and more willing to assume responsibilities for their own health and welfare.

Government intervention in areas of the mind, taste, and judgment has always been ineffective without popular support. When self-reliance and independent judgment become harmonious principles related to the education of everyone, a government role in regulating or censoring schools, newsstands, television, radio, or movies will diminish. Individual humanitarian responsibility will be the accepted answer to any question of government or other censorship. An increased awareness of and proximity to a real world will dampen the very urge to censor.

A thirty-hour work week, retirement at 55, and an average life expectancy beyond 80 will help make the media curriculum a necessity. In formal schooling, the individual citizen will have developed within himself resources of mind and spirit that will make him dependent primarily upon himself, with his life centered upon cultural and intellectual interests. Study for profit and study for pleasure will be one, and the meaning of the word "school" will revert more to its original Greek meaning, *leisure*. The idea of education as something to be strained for by plodding back and forth to school and enduring painful hours of classes patrolled by professional educators will be dismissed. Rather than being a forbidding chore, education will be an inviting challenge, like climbing mountains or catching fish. People will develop a genuine pleasure in learning, in a sense, making it as far removed from suffering as health is from sickness. The influences of family, the media, work, and the community will combine with the educational institution to form an enjoyable learning opportunity for persons of all ages.[37] Modern dilemmas in understanding the difference between an education that is wanted and one that is unwanted will vanish.

The enjoyment will include laughter. Teachers, students, and administrators alike will laugh more and do so with spontaneity. They will laugh at themselves, at pomposity, and at society. Comedy will thrive. There will be amusement, but not derision, at such overly serious learning-teaching behavior as has been described by novelist George Eliot: "It is an uneasy lot at best, to be what we call highly taught and yet not to enjoy; to be present at this great spectacle of life and never to be liberated from a small, hungry, shivering self."[38] As will be true of education, laughter will be an experience to be shared with everyone. Therefore, it will never descend to mockery for as one social analyst has written, "Ridicule makes us inferiors. Only equals can laugh and tease together."[39] Perhaps one might anticipate that the 90 million people who laugh daily at the "Peanuts" comic strips are already being prepared for the new look at learning.

Educational institutions themselves, of course, will continue to vary widely. One campus may be prominent in preparing the future scientist, technician, or physician. Another will occupy itself more with philosophy and offering education to teachers, lawyers, religious workers, and political aspirants. A third college may be known for the social understanding it enhances. Many institutions will have programs of travel, field trips, sports, useful community service, interning, and other so-called paracurricular ventures in increasing variety, for these are also a part of liberal learning. Administrators will have no need to debate the position of the student who wrote to the editor of *Look* magazine: "What the Establishment can't grasp is that you can get a better education from two years with VISTA or the Peace Corps than from four years in your major universities."[40] As a matter of principle, educators who are media-oriented will lead in making cooperative endeavors of these kinds of projects.

The student will understand the difficulty of equating every kind of adventure and service with sound curricular requirements and evaluation systems. He will be pleased at clarification of the kind of semidirect experience that is afforded by the mass media. Rather than being mere prerequisites to a specific vocation, programs of general studies and liberal arts schools will promote intrinsic and abiding values, freedom and discipline for the mind to grasp the fullness of knowledge, as well as a sense of continuing responsibility for the mass media. Listening groups, such as are characteristic of a more direct democracy in many countries,[41] will meet regularly and with broader cultural and personal fulfillment. Adult and continuing education programs, continuation classes, and post-graduate courses will proliferate.

The two-year junior or community college will thrive as a college rather than as a trade or vocational-technical school. Recognizing the need of a general-liberal foundation to all education, the supporters of the state junior colleges already have left open the possibility of development into four-year institutions in many instances. The campus will instill a built-in spirit of continuing education that is self-propelled. Education will become less dependent upon escalating public funds, and an entirely new economic base will be used in projecting the costs of higher education.

The motives for attending college will hardly be new, but they will sharpen in clarity for more people. Whether thinking of his goal primarily as vocational preparation or as liberal-general understanding, the student will find neither glorified at the expense of the other. A well-prepared professional or a tradesman will cherish his liberal-general educational background as highly as a graduate in liberal arts will come to respect the pursuit of any occupation that is beneficial to humanity.

Disillusionment with high school or college will diminish. Student rebellion will vanish. Their recrudescence will be a rhetoric of trust among all concerned, the symmetry of learning and teaching. Academic administration will have long abandoned the suppression of student unrest, dissent, or involvement in controversial issues. Instead, students will receive positive guidance in the search for ways to improve society. Any dropouts will be given second, third, and fourth chances, especially those from a former time when the strength of their self-motivation, self-discipline, and self-study was overshadowed by rigid classroom procedures. Stopouts will be encouraged: students will spend a year or more away from school in a learning experience.

Tomorrow's student will not be wedged between the two conflicting revolutions of education and the mass media, but he will understand both. He will not be Renaissance Man, for today's explosion of knowledge has made it impossible for one person to study everything, and today's democracy has made education available for the millions beyond the relatively few of any medieval aristocracy. Ridded of schizophrenia, the student will be a Modern Man who knows that true education must have meaningful direction, personal challenge, and sound discipline and that its milieu can continue properly and unendingly for everyone via the mass media.

No longer will there be the "crisis in the classroom" that was described by Charles Silberman, author of the book of the same title. The conclusions he made before a national teachers' meeting held the hope of schools [that will] "be humane and still educate well, . . . that will be genuinely concerned with gaiety and joy and individual growth and fulfillment without sacrificing concern for intellectual discipline and development, . . . be simultaneously child-centered and subject- or knowledge-centered, . . . [stressing] aesthetic and moral education without weakening the three R's."[42]

In the future, intellectual endeavor will be as possible and as respectable outside the classroom as within it. The serious student will have every opportunity to be strong and worthy before he comes to the campus. After he leaves, he will neither need nor desire the label of "college graduate" as a status symbol. The alumnus most loyal will no longer be lost in the mists of the long-forgotten ceremony, the grand ballroom, or the football field. He may continue to enjoy the athletic victories of the alma mater, but they will not overshadow the academic achievements and the intellectual and ethical contributions of the campus. Like stockholders in a corporation, alumni will still invest in their alma maters, but they will be drawing richer dividends from all of higher education. They will identify with the meaning that traverses education at all levels.

The citizen without a college education will suffer neither insolent reproach nor social handicap. Already on the wane for reasons of economic and political change, the "Every-Man-A-College-Degree" philosophy will have totally vanished. Those who would have been perfectly happy as farmers or clerks will no longer feel forced to strive to be something they are not. Education will emphasize sensitivity and appreciation but leave the creativity to come of itself untarnished. Then it will be said that to be uneducated is to be insensitive and, in some circumstances, immoral. Remaining uneducated will be worse than being unemployed in the face of opportunity to work.

Instead of seeing a college career as a privilege enjoyed only by some, people will speak of an educational commitment as the responsibility of all. The need will continue for student-centered schools designed to prepare youth to serve in many occupations, but the new media curriculum will help to meet the crying need for the education-centered community. This community will be "one that lives and breathes education, a community in which business, the church, the mass media, and the vast number of voluntary agencies that pepper and salt the landscape of America, are all mobilized for educational purposes."[43]

Maurice Fabre, a Swiss historian, wrote: "It is possible to foresee the day when all the media of communication, from books through television to computers and teaching machines, will harmoniously combine to instruct as well as to entertain the broad mass of citizens around the world."[44]

Professional education will be the leading social force to counteract the technomania of gadgetry with all of it pushbuttons, conversion boxes, outputs, screens and feedbacks that transmit only shadows, whether the gadgetry is located in a media room at home or a media center on campus. It will prevent futuristic inventions from stifling the human race with passivity and dependence, from mounting beyond human control. The teacher will provide the leadership that will keep the technology practical and steer it in directions for human progress.

The educator will nurture and fill the role of warm companionship and interpersonal contact that are technologically impossible for the mass media. This will be a relationship with all learners among the entire citizenry. Together, teacher and learner will explore, develop, and improve the abundance of educational content and the potential of public communications. Leaders and personalities among the mass media will find their essential complementation in professional educators. The liberal-general goals of education will mesh with the dramatic techniques of the media for the millions. Citizens will respond by making education a normal part of their daily lives.

These bold prognostications are not mere utopian ideals. They are as serious as the hopes expressed in any commencement address, as expectant as the endeavors of mass advertisers, as open-eyed as the deserving students who earnestly strive to be educated. The hopes are as honest and practical as education itself. Kenneth Keniston in his book, *The Uncommitted*[45] argued: "The Utopian impulse runs deep in all human life, and especially deep in American life. What is needed is to free that impulse once again to redirect it toward the creation of a better society." If futurologists can prophesy gloom and doom—and be wrong—at least educators can learn from the publicity that the mass media have so often given to a dismal tomorrow—and hope to be accurate with their optimism.

Rather than to patch up threadbare values and outworn purposes, people will aspire beyond the vistas of mere technology and dare to construct a society more fully human for everyone. It is under the conditions of this kind of challenge for tomorrow that the colleges and universities, their teachers, students, and alumni can and will be respected for leadership in fostering what former University of Chicago President William Rainey Harper called "the work of the prophet, the priest, and the philosopher of democracy."[46]

9

SYMMETRY OF WISDOM WITHOUT END

Education in a democracy stands today before its most harrowing crises. As a means of transmitting the culture, it has always connoted uplift and enlightenment, essentials that are quite apart from the mere prolongation of an intellectual and moral status quo. In its general-liberal phase, education has had basic or implied distinctions from occupational or terminal training for wages. Education means the knowledge and thought of wisdom. Inherent in the concept of education is the goal of broadening and liberating the mind in a sense wherein it is ever without termination, for the mind of man as an image of the mind of Creation is without limits.

A democracy is based on constitutional provisions and humanitarian principles of freedom, equality, and responsibility. The cultivation and expression of knowledge and thought are similarly the right and obligation of everyone. Understanding and appreciation of the human struggle for enlightenment are not the monopoly of a single class or group. Education as the opportunity for individual development and humanitarian wisdom must belong to everyone, or eventually it will come to belong to no one. In this sense, education is unending in that countless numbers and combinations of people are its audience.

In a modern democracy, education is disseminated through two main channels: public communications and the campus. The offerings of the former—television, radio, movies, recordings, newspapers, magazines, and paperbacks—are inescapable for nearly everyone. The offerings of the schools—programs of instruction in prescribed subject matter or methodologies—are easily avoided outside the classroom. Both channels are allied to a modern revolution in life-styles. Both share the potential for a symmetry of wisdom without end.

But the purpose and effect of the one diverge from and often conflict with the other. A system of public communications, largely commercial in sponsorship, is highly democratic in its purpose and effect. Huge audiences numbering in the millions are essential to its existence. If necessary to attract them, the mass media settle for the lowest common denominator of popular values and culture, an action that may not drag the quality down, but also does not deliberately point it upward. The focus is always massive, and it is reaching the populace at a revolutionary pace.

A liberal-general education has as an avowed purpose: the elevation of the human race and stimulation of individuals to further development. Its stress is on freeing the mind and body to absorb the breadth of culture and the depth of knowledge, and applying the resulting wisdom and ability to human service. The liberally educated intellect has played an important part in every revolutionary movement that has advanced human enlightenment. It understands the need to pace and control revolutions.

Today's vocationally oriented campus has veered from liberal-general education. Overwhelmingly, technical training and occupational goals are stressed. The curriculum is unduly restricted; it stresses professional specialization even in liberal arts fields. Schools of higher learning withdraw and even isolate themselves from the ordinary citizen. In meeting the challenge or crisis of increasing education for all classes, races, and groups in the population, the strict classroom system proceeds at a lagging pace. It is incapable of forwarding the dream of universal education.

For untold numbers of college and high school students, including those in programs of liberal arts and general studies, education means disillusionment or superficiality. It has no purposeful end because it has no meaningful framework. It rests only as facade. Classroom walls, specialized courses, and routine assignments have constricted the life spirit of education for which, in turn, instructors themselves have often been the midwives who delivered in a stillborn condition.

Meanwhile the mass media quicken their pace and set the stage for an eventual marriage with education. They visualize educator-communicators who will direct centers of learning, illuminate the values of American life, both the false and the true, and instruct and lead the people into a less anxious and more rewarding way of living.[1] They pour out their abundance of culture in response to popular demand; they entertain and inform the millions. The media can rekindle the embers of education for disillusioned students and expand the glow into enlightenment. The students can find intellectual liberation and stimulation in a significant movie, recording, broadcast, magazine article, newspaper editorial, or paperback that received no mention or reference whatsoever in the classroom. Like many other citizens, they cannot comprehend why so many liberal-general study proclamations come from the college platform and so few from the mass media.

The observer of education in action also ponders the impossibility that the school or campus alone can cope with the task it must always assume. To educate everyone means more than the enticing of youth and the inviting of adults to enroll in classes for lectures or discussion. A faith in the capacity of education to solve our problems and advance the human race cannot reside in an outside force. It must be a resolve of people to educate themselves from within. The task implacably beckons the aid of massive public communications. The call is loud for a new attitude toward schooling, one that incorporates a new media power concept of education.

The objectives and values of knowledge, wisdom, and human kindness are well established in existing courses in college, high school, and elementary school. The professional educator and the public communicator need only join forces to make them realizable for everyone. The transition to a curriculum that embraces the mass media can be made imperceptibly. The effect can be lasting and will occur, as soon as responsible self-realization, teaching and learning for action, and mass media improvement become realities. The direct operative influence of the high school and college curriculum of liberal arts and general studies will have no bounds.

The power to see through the present into the future is similar to the poet's keen perception of human nature and the human situation. The technology and the system, the hardware and the regulations to communicate are in marked evidence almost everywhere. The visibility for noble purpose, however, is murky and overcast. Must one lament that "no modern equivalent of the Beowulf poet now tells of a man who struggles, in age as in youth, to save his people from destruction"?[2] If so, let one note that modern times are for the millions and that salvation will come by transforming media concern from fetish to vision-making, from nightmare to enlightenment, from present imperfection to improvement for the morrow.

How much of the unending picture of tomorrow's wisdom will ever come into focus? Obviously, no one knows. But much of it is unfolding and inevitable; some of it is urgent; and most of it is desirable. The assertions of a preview and challenge for tomorrow are not parody or false utopia. The mind of modern man has an unprecedented amount of time during which it is left free to absorb almost anything offered it. Unless people learn what is right to think and do, the freedom of either thinking or doing has little significance. The college student is no exception. Citizens of a democratic nation must act on the conviction that wisdom should be filling minds of all human beings.

Formal education needs the mass media if it is to survive; the mass media need educational leadership if they are to progress. The problem is one of bridging the gap between them. The mass media offer the possibility of open-ended wisdom for everyone. They are filled with entertainment and information from which the college campus can select and propagate that which is truly human. The campus can influence, guide, and supplement the media offerings. Given the prospects of greater cooperation between the two principal channels, we are certain to help more people find "the wisdom we have lost in knowledge and the knowledge we have lost in information,"[3] which the poetry of T. S. Eliot so beautifully praises.

NOTES

Chapter 1: Nightmare and Fetish

1. Bernard Rosenberg and others, comp., *Mass Society in Crisis, Social Problems and Social Pathology*, 2nd ed., New York, Macmillan, 1971.
2. George Wald, "Arise, Ye Prisoners of Extinction," *Intellect*, April 1976, p. 501.
3. See also "Understanding Marshall McLuhan," or, "Will TV Put a Zombie in Your Future?" *Senior Scholastic*, April 18, 1967, p. 16.
4. *Ibid.*
5. Arthur Schlesinger, "Is Gutenberg Dead?" in *Mass Communication; Selected Readings for Librarians*, K.J. Mc Garry, ed., Hamden, Conn., Linnet Books, 1972, pp. 133-134.

Chapter 2: Educational Schizophrenia

1. H.L. Mencken, *Prejudices: Fifth Series*, Knopf, 1926, p. 177.
2. Robert L. Stevenson, "An Apology for Idlers," in *Travels and Essays*, Scribner, 1909, p. 69.
3. *Cf.* David Mallery, *Ferment on the Campus; An Encounter with the New College Generation*, New York: Harper, 1966, p. 3.
4. E. Lee McLean, in American Association of State College and Universities Proceedings, 10th Annual Meeting, 1970, p. 37.
5. A considerable portion of this section was first developed by the author for an article entitled, "Schizophrenia in Becoming Educated," *School and Society*, 1960, pp. 461-63.
6. *Teaching by Television*, New York, Ford Foundation and Fund for the Advancement of Education, 1959, p. 3.
7. "Heere's the Prof . . .," *Time*, Dec. 2, 1974, p. 92.
8. "Princeton 56," as criticized by Henry Mitchell in the *Commercial Appeal*, Memphis, May 21, 1956.
9. Jonathan Miller, *Marshall McLuhan*, New York, Viking, 1971, p. 2.
10. Robert Sidwell, "The Medium is Mostly Tedium," *Phi Delta Kappan*, Jan. 1973 pp. 322-323.
11. Frank Stanton, "Remarks," Ninth General Conference of CBS Television Network Affiliates, New York, 1963, p. 2.
12. Philip Jones, "Educational TV in Your Schools may be Anything but Educational." *American School Board Journal*, March 1974, pp. 25-28. Robert MacNeil, "Twenty-five Years of Public Television Have Been Filled with Promise, Prestige and Problems," *TV Guide*, March 18, 1978.
13. Ralph Thompson, "Viaticum for Life: Comments on General Education," *Improving College and University Teaching*, Autumn 1974, p. 247.

14. Marshall McLuhan, *The Medium Is the Message* New York: Bantam Books, 1967, p. 18.

15. Robert Hilliard, "Media and Education. A look at it like it is," Speech, Washington, D.C., Association for Supervision and Curriculum Development, June 7, 1968.

16. Harold L. Wilensky, "Mass Society and Mass Culture: Interdependence or Independence?" in *American Sociological Review*, April 1964, p. 196.

17. William C. Hodapp, "American Inventory," in *A Television Policy for Education*, ed. by Carroll V. Newsom, Washington, American Council on Education, 1952, p. 56.

18. Quoted in "Book Learning and Barricades," *Chicago Tribune Book World*, August 4, 1968, p. 5.

19. Malcolm G. Scully, "Inflated Grades Worrying More and More Colleges," *Chronicle of Higher Education*, May 19, 1975, p., 1 and Roger B. May, "A Glut of A's and B's has Phi Beta Kappa Looking to its Laurels," *Wall Street Journal*, May 23, 1975, p. 1.

20. J. B. Priestly, "Mostly about Nothing," *New Statesman*, March 3, 1967, p. 289.

21. Alan Abelson, "Up and Down Wall Street," *Barron's National Business Weekly*, May 12, 1975, p. 1.

Chapter 3: A REVOLUTION TOO SWIFT—COMMUNICATIONS

1. Cf. Jose Ortega y Gasset, *The Revolt of the Masses*, London, Allen and Unwin, 1932.

2. Don R. Pember, *Mass Media in America*, New York, Science Research Associates, 1974, p. 1.

3. John Bradshaw, "The Shape of Media Things to Come (A Science-Fiction Story That's All True)," *New York Magazine*, April 19, 1976, p. 63.

4. Maurice B. Mitchell, "A Forward Look at Communications, Feature Article," *Britannica Book of the Year, 1958*, Chicago, Encyclopedia Britannica, 1958, pp. 49–64.

5. Joan Kron, "The Media Room," *New York Magazine*, April 19, 1976, p. 55.

6. Robert Stein, *Media Power, Who is Shaping your Picture of the World?*, Boston, Houghton Mifflin, 1972, p. 236.

7. See Lydia Strong, "They're Selling Your Unconscious," *Saturday Review*, November 13, 1954, p. 11.

8. Arthur A. Houghton, "Leisure Time and the Liberal Arts," *Association of American Colleges Bulletin*, December 1953, p. 620.

9. For an elaboration on the government's historical relations with communications, see Zachariah Chafee, Jr., *Government and Mass Communications*, Chicago, University of Chicago Press, 1947, Vol. 1; Fred S. Siebert et al. *Four Theories of the Press*, Urbana, U. of Illinois Press, 1956; and Commission on Freedom of the Press, *A Free and Responsible Press*, Chicago, University of Chicago Press, 1947, chapters 1 and 2.

10. The political manipulation of communications has been documented in many authoritative studies. See *Communications and Political Development*, ed. by Lucian W. Pye, Princeton, Princeton University Press, 1963, pp. 238-41, 254-69; Jay W. Stein, "The Soviet Intelligentsia," *Russian Review*, October 1951, pp. 283-92; "The Soviet Librarian," *Library Journal*, February 1952, pp. 164-67; Mark W. Hopkins, "Media, Party, and Society in Russia," in Allan Wells, ed., *Mass Communications, A World View*, Palo Alto, California, National Press, 1974, p. 45.

11. Cf. John Hulteng and Roy Nelson, *The Fourth Estate, an Informal Appraisal of the News and Opinion Media*, New York, Harper and Row, 1971, pp. 235-238.

12. Philip L. Geyelin and Douglas Cater, *American Media: Adequate or Not?*, Washington, D.C., American Enterprise Institute for Public Policy Research, 1970, p. 67.

13. Robert Cirino, *Don't Blame the People, How the News Media use Bias, Distortion and Censorship to Manipulate Public Opinion*, Los Angeles, Diversity Press, 1971, p. 69.

14. Newton N. Minow, John B. Martin, and Lee M. Mitchell, *Presidential Television*, New York, Basic Books, 1973, p. 11.

15. Nicholas Johnson, "The Media Barons and the Public Interest," in John Stevens and William Porter *The Rest of the Elephant, Perspectives on the Mass Media*, Englewood Cliffs, Prentice-Hall, 1973, p. 55.

16. Rene Maheu, "The Intruders," *UNESCO Courier*, February 1967, p. 23.

17. Carl L. Becker, *Freedom and Responsibility in the American Way of Life*, New York, Knopf, 1945, pp. 62-63.

18. *Education for Public Responsibility*, A statement by the Directors of the Fund for Adult Education, White Plains, New York, 1959, p. 10.

19. Wilbur Schramm, "Mass Communication," in George A. Miller, ed., *Communication, Language, and Meaning; Psychological Perspectives*, New York, Basic Books, 1973, p. 222.

20. Quoted in David G. Clark, and William B. Blankenburg, *You and Media; Mass Communication and Society*, San Francisco, Canfield Press, 1973, p. 126.

21. H. Carleton Greene, "Address at the 1962 Dupont Awards Foundation Dinner," Washington, D.C. quoted in *Journalism Quarterly*, Autumn 1962, p. 444.

22. Cf. Melvin DeFleur, *Theories of Mass Communication*, New York, David McKay, 1970, p. 156–57.

23. Maheu, *op. cit.*, p. 24.

24. Pyke Johnson, Jr., "The Distribution of Paperbound Books," *ALA Bulletin*, June 1963, p. 534. Clarence Peterson, *The Bantam Story, Thirty Years of Paperback Publishing*, New York, Bantam, 1975.

25. Edmund Carpenter, *O, What a Blow That Phantom Gave Me*, Holt, Rinehart, and Winston, 1974, p. 3.

26. Robert Bishop and Helen Johnson, "Magazine Treatment of Report," *Columbia Journalism Review*, Fall 1968, p. 53.

27. "Telling the Tape Tale," *Newsweek*, May 13, 1974, p. 136.

28. Cf. George I. Gropper, "Why *is* a Picture Worth a Thousand Words," *Audio-Visual Communication Review*, July-August 1963, p. 94.

29. Pitrim A. Sorokin, *The Crisis of Our Age, The Social and Cultural Outlook*, New York, Dutton, 1942, p. 67.

30. H. A. Overstreet, "What We Read, See and Hear," in *The Mature Mind*, New York Norton, 1949, p. 204.

31. Frank Stanton, *Television and People*. New York, Columbia Broadcasting System, 1949, p. 19.

32. Moses Hadas, *Old Wine, New Bottles, A Humanist Teacher at Work*, New York, Simon and Schuster, 1962, p. 136.

33. James S. Smith, "Simultaneousness," *English Journal*, May 1968, p. 698.

34. Cited in Shirley Winston, "Children and the Mass Media," *Children*, Nov.-Dec. 1970, p. 242.

35. David Sarnoff, "Education in Our World of Change," *Teachers College Record*, Oct. 1960, p. 66.

36. Douglas Cater, "Communications Policy Research: The Need for New Definitions," in William L. Rivers and William T. Slater, *Aspen Handbook on the Media: Research, Publications, Organizations*, Palo Alto, Cal., Aspen Program on Communications and Society, 1973, p. x.

37. Herbert A. Schiller, "Towards a Democratic Reconstruction of Mass Communications; The Social Use of Technology," in Richard Hixon, ed. *Mass Media: A Casebook*, New York, Crowell, 1973, p. 69-70.

38. Quoted in "Communication as a Fermenting Agent — a Keynote View," SDC Magazine, May 1967, p. 4.

39. Henry D. Thoreau, *Walden*, Boston, Houghton, Osgood, 1879, p. 57.

40. Brenda Maddox, *Beyond Babel; New Directions in Communications*, New York, Simon and Schuster, 1972, p. 16.

Chapter 4: A REVOLUTION TOO MILD—EDUCATION

1. Jose Ortega y Gasset, *The Modern Theme*, New York, Norton, 1933, p. 101.

2. Alan Toffler, *Future Shock*, New York, Random House, 1970.

3. Crane Brinton, *The Anatomy of Revolution*, New York, Norton, 1938, p. 301.

4. Francis Keppel, *The Necessary Revolution in American Education*, New York, Harper, 1966, p. 1.

5. Mortimer J. Adler and Milton Mayer, *The Revolution in Education*, Chicago, University of Chicago Press, 1958, p. 195.

6. John Seeley. "Youth in Revolt; Special Report," in *Britannica Book of the Year*, 1969, p. 315; and Leonard Buckley, "Education," in *Britannica Book of the Year*, 1971, p. 297.

7. "Panorama," *Chicago Daily News*, June 15, 1968.

8. Logan Wilson, ed., *Patterns in American Higher Education*, Washington, D.C., American Council on Education, 1965.

9. Donald J. Cowling and Carter Davidson, *Colleges for Freedom, A Study of Purposes, Practices, and Needs*, New York, Harper, 1947, p. 51.

10. *Higher Education for American Democracy*, A Report of the President's Commission on Higher Education, Washington, 1947, vol. 1, p. 49.

11. Jacques Barzun, *College to University—and After*, Address at the Convocation celebrating the first year of Hofstra's existence as a university, December 11, 1963, p. 7.

12. Rufus E. Miles, Jr., "The Search for Identity of Graduate Schools of Public Affairs," *Public Adminstration Review*, November 1967, pp. 343-56.

13. Catherine Marshall, "The Gordian Knot of Education," *Association of American Colleges Bulletin*, March 1955, p. 27.

14. Theodore M. Hesburgh, "Liberal Education in the World Today," *Association of American Colleges Bulletin*, March 1955, pp. 86-7.

15. Alvin C. Eurich, "The Commitment to Experiment and Innovate in College Teaching," *Educational Record*, Winter 1964, p. 51.

16. Frank Aydelotte, *Breaking the Academic Lockstep*, New York, Harper, 1944, p. 14.

17. William S. Learned, *Credits versus Education*, Reprinted from the Proceedings of the Associated Academic Principals of the State of New York, 1933.

18. Maurice L. Jacks, *Total Education, A Plea for Synthesis*, London, Kegan Paul, 1946, p. 53.

19. Joseph K. Hart, *A Social Interpretation of Education*, New York, Holt, 1929, p. xviii.

20. Paul Heist, ed., *The Creative College Student: An Unmet Challenge*, San Francisco, Jossey-Bass, 1968, p. 53.

21. Cf. George F. Budd, "The Image of Teacher Education as Reflected in the Mass Media," 15th yearbook of the American Association of Colleges for Teacher Education, Washington, 1962, pp. 50-3; and Ted Klein and Fred Danzig, *How to be Heard; Making the Media Work for You*, New York, Macmillan, 1974.

22. Newton and Nell Minow, "What are We Learning from Television?" *Change*, October 1976, p. 48.

23. Alfred Whitehead, *The Aims of Education and Other Essays*, New York, Macmillan, 1929, p. 10.

24. Paul L. Mackendrick, "Some Thoughts on Humanists and the Mass Media," *American Council of Learned Societies Newsletter*, Fall 1956, p. 9.

25. Betty B. Franks and Mary K. Howard, "Thinking Futures," *Media and Methods*, Nov. 1974, p. 29.

26. James Cass, "The Crisis of Confidence and Beyond," *Saturday Review*, Sept. 19, 1970, p. 61.

27. *General Education in a Free Society*, Report of the Harvard Committee, Cambridge, Harvard University Press, 1945, p. 30.

28. Ralf Brent, "Education by Electronics," *Vital Speeches*, January 1, 1966, p. 178.

29. Robert Lindsay and Raymond B. Nixon, "Two Decades in the World of the Mass Media," *UNESCO Courier*, July–August 1966, p. 37.

30. "The Assassination," *Columbia Journalism Review*, Winter 1963, p. 5.

Chapter 5: Teaching for Learning, Formal and Informal

1. William H. Burton, *The Guidance of Learning Activities*, New York, Appleton-Century-Crofts, 2nd. ed., 1952, Ch. 7.

2. Henry Adams, *The Education of Henry Adams, An Autobiography*, Boston, Houghton Mifflin, 1918, p. 300.

3. B. F. Skinner, "Are Theories of Learning Necessary?" *Psychological Review*, July 1952, pp. 193-216.

4. Arthur R. King, Jr., and John A. Brownell, *The Curriculum and the Disciplines of Knowledge*, New York, Wiley, 1966, pp. 106-107, and Glenn L. Snelbecker, *Learning Theory, Instructional Theory, and Psychoeducational Design*, New York, McGraw Hill, 1974, p. 13.

5. For detailed analyses of learning factors, see G. Lester Anderson and Arthur I. Gates, "The General Nature of Learning," in the *49th Yearbook of the National Society for the Study of Education*, Chicago, University of Chicago Press, 1950, pt. 1, pp. 12–35; Richard J. Mueller, *Principles of Classroom Learning and Perception*, New York, 1974; and John A. R. Wilson et al, *Psychological Foundations of Learning and Teaching*, New York, McGraw-Hill, 1969. Some of the accounts in this chapter were presented by the author in "Public Communications and Educational Psychology," *North Central Association Quarterly*, Spring, 1970, pp. 352-60.

6. Cf. Albert Rapp, "The Experimental Background of Problems of Learning," *Classical Journal*, May 1945, pp. 479–80.

7. Quoted in *Wall Street Journal*, May 13, 1976, p. 16.

8. See Barry McLaughlin, *Learning and Social Behavior*, New York, Free Press, 1971, chapter 4, and Neal E. Miller and John Dollard, *Social Learning and Imitation*, New Haven, Yale University Press, 1941, pp. 307-310.

9. Franklin Fearing, "Social Impact of the Mass Media of Communication," in *53rd Yearbook of the National Society for the Study of Education*, Chicago, University of Chicago Press, 1954, pt. 2, p. 183.

10. Søren Kierkegaard, *Repetition; an Essay in Experimental Psychology*, tr. by Walter Lowrie, New York, Harper, 1941, p. 34.

11. *Wall Street Journal*, May 5, 1976, p. 20.

12. Harold Mendelsohn, "Socio-psychological Perspectives on the Mass Media and Public Anxiety," *Journalism Quarterly*, Autumn 1963, p. 515.

13. William James, *Psychology*, New York, Holt, 1890, vol. I, p. 127.

14. Max McConn, *College or Kindergarten*, New York, New Republic, 1928, pp. 18–23.

15. Aristotle, *Politics*, tr. by Benjamin Jowett, Oxford, 1923, p. 307.

16. Jay Haley, "The Appeal of the Moving Pictures," *Quarterly of Film, Radio and Television*, Summer 1952, p. 368.

17. Joseph K. Hart, *A Social Interpretation of Education*, New York, Holt, 1929, pp. 225-226.

18. *Liberal Education Re-examined, Its Role in a Democracy*, New York, Harper, 1943, p. 89.

19. Cf., William I. Thomas, "The Configurations of Personality," in *The Unconscious, a Symposium*, New York, Knopf, 1927, Ch. 6.

20. Elihu Katz and David Foulkes, "On the Use of the Mass Media as Escape: Clarification of a Concept," *Public Opinion Quarterly*, Fall 1962, p. 379.

21. Erik Barnouw, *Mass Communication; Television, Radio, Film, Press; The Media and Their Practice in the United States*, New York, Rinehart, 1956, p. 70.

22. K. B. Madsen, *Modern Theories of Motivation*, New York, Wiley, 1974, p. 307.

23. *The College Creative Student; An Unmet Challenge*, quoted in Paul Heist, ed., San Francisco, Jossey-Bass, 1968, p. 53.

24. Nathaniel Cantor and Stephen Corey, *The Teaching Learning Process*, New York, Dryden, 1953. p. 4.

25. David Gelman, "The 'Contagion' Issue," *Newsweek*, Oct. 6, 1975, pp. 77-78.

26. Wilbur Schramm, *Men, Messages and Media; A Look at Human Communication*, New York, Harper and Row, 1973, p. 194.

Chapter 6: HARNESSING THE POWER OF THE MASS MEDIA

1. Harold D. Lasswell, "The Structure and Function of Communication in Society," in *The Communication of Ideas*, ed. by Lyman Bryson, New York, Harper, 1948, p. 37.

2. Joseph T. Klapper, *The Effects of Mass Communication*, Glencoe, Illinois, Free Press, 1960, p. 48.

3. Wilbur L. Schramm, *Men, Messages, and Media* New York, Harper and Row, 1973, ch. 10.

4. George Washington, quoted on a calendar.

5. A. Donald Brice, *Writing Out Loud, A Hintful Handbook for Dictators*, New York, Dictaphone, 1957, p. 2.

6. Winston L. Brembeck and William S. Howell, *Persuasion, A Means of Social Control*, New York, Prentice-Hall, 1952, pp. 165-82.

7. *Cf.* Dorwin Cartwright, "Some Principles of Mass Persuasion," in *Dimensions of Communication*, ed. by Lee Richardson, New York, Appleton-Century-Crofts, 1969, ch. 12.

8. Brembeck, *op. cit.*, pp. 183–84.

9. Charles S. Steinberg, *The Mass Communicators: Public Relations, Public Opinion, and Mass Media*, New York, Harper and Row, 1958, p. 162.

10. Dwight D. MacDonald, "A Theory of Mass Culture," in *Mass Culture, the Popular Arts in America*, ed. by Bernard Rosenberg and David M. White, Glencoe, Illinois, Free Press, 1957, p. 72.

11. "Report," published April 1966 by Fund for the Republic's Center for the Study of Democratic Institutions, *Newsweek*, May 2, 1966.

12. Carl Henry, "Where is Television Going?" *Christianity Today*, October 11, 1974, p. 42.

13. Harold Orlans, "Public Pornography," *Dissent*, Winter 1954, p. 107.

14. G. Harry Nelson, "To Dam the Tide," Letter to Editor, *Christianity Today*, Dec., 1961, p. 15.

15. Perry C. Cotham, *Obscenity, Pornography, and Censorship*, Grand Rapids, Mich., Baker Book House, 1973, p. 35.

16. Margaret Culkin Banning, quoted in Jay Walz, "Writer Cites Way to Fight Obscenity," *New York Times*, Dec. 4, 1952, p. 26.

17. Frederic Wertham and Harris Peck, respectively, quoted in Sophia M. Robinson, *Juvenile Delinquency, Its Nature and Control*, New York, Holt, Rinehart and Winston, 1961, pp. 156–57.

18. Norbert Muhlen, "Comic Books and Other Horrors: Prep-School for Totalitarian Society?" *Commentary*, Jan.–March 1949, p. 87.

19. W. W. Charters, *Motion Pictures and Youth, A Summary*, Payne Fund Studies, New York, Macmillan, 1933, pp. 54, 60.

20. Bill Diehl, Entertainment Editor of *St. Paul Dispatch*, quoted by Jenkin L. Jones, "Who is Tampering with the Soul of America," speech before American Society of Newspaper Editors, mimeo, n.d.

21. Cotham, *op. cit.*, p. 25.

22. An essayist and novelist quoted in Frank Stanton, *Television and People*, New York, Columbia Broadcasting System, 1949, p. 14.

23. Gene Klavan, *Turn that Damned Thing Off; An Irreverent Look at TV's Impact on the American Scene*, Indianapolis, Bobbs-Merrill, 1972, p. 49.

24. Kenneth G. Bartlett, "Social Impact of the Radio," in *Communication and Social Action*, Annals of the American Academy of Political and Social Science, March 1947, p. 97.

25. Gary A. Steiner, *The People Look at Television, A Study of Audience Attitudes*, New York, Knopf, 1963, p. 94.

26. Fred Allen, quoted in "Old Timer," *Time*, August 31, 1953, p. 60.

27. Penn Kimball, "Can we communicate with Europe?" *Saturday Review*, July 8, 1967, p. 55.

28. Peter M. Sandman and others, *Media, An Introductory Analysis of American Mass Communications*, Englewood Cliffs, N.J., Prentice Hall, 1972.

29. Quoted in Charles A. Siepmann, *Television and Education in the United States*, Paris, UNESCO, 1952, p. 12.

30. Eliot A. Daly, "Is TV Brutalizing Your Child?" *Look Magazine*, Dec. 2, 1969, p. 99.

31. "To Establish Justice, To Insure Domestic Tranquility," Final Report of the National Commission on the Causes and Prevention of Violence, Washington, D.C., 1969.

32. Jerzy Kosinski, "A Nation of Videots," *Media & Methods*, April 1975, p. 5.

33. Statistics reported at the 1971 National Convention of the American Academy of Pediatrics, cited in *The Media: Persuasion, Propaganda, and Power*, A Campus Communications Kit, New York, Scholastic, 1975.

34. Charles G. Wrenn and D. L. Harley, *Time on Their Hands, A Report on Leisure, Recreation, and Young People*, Washington, American Council on Education, 1941, p. 27.

35. Frederic Wertham, quoted in Victor B. Cline, ed. *Where do you Draw the Line; an Exploration into Media Violence, Pornography, and Censorship*, Provo, Utah, Brigham Young University Press, 1974, p. 166.

36. Ralph E. Lapp, *Kill and Overkill; the Strategy of Annihilation*, New York, Basic Books, 1962, p. 154.

37. Otto N. Larsen, ed., *Violence and the Mass Media*, New York, Harper and Row, 1968, p. 282.

38. Frances Hennoch, quoted in Frederic Wertham, "How Movie and TV Violence Affect Children," *Ladies Home Journal*, Feb. 1960, p. 166.

39. Karl Jaspers, *Tragedy is Not Enough*, Boston, Beacon Press, 1952, p. 36.

40. Dan Lacy, *Freedom and Communications*, Urbana, University of Illinois Press, 1961, p. 76.

41. "Move is Under Way in Britain to Dilute Strong Liquor Ads," *Wall Street Journal*, April 19, 1976.

42. Marilynn Preston, "Is Prime Time TV Tuning Itself out by Turning on to Drink?" *Chicago Tribune*, March 30, 1976, p. 17.

43. "Combining all Channels to Reach a Mass Public," *Business Week*, Sept. 18, 1965 pp. 80–88.

44. John Keats, *The Crack in the Picture Window*, Boston, Houghton Mifflin, 1956, p. 193.

45. Ernest Van den Haag, Lecture at the Footprints VIII Conference, Reported in *Syracuse Daily Orange*, March 10, 1961.

46. "Glorification of Violence," *Christian Century*, Oct. 8, 1975, p. 868.

47. Otto N. Larsen, *op. cit.*, p. 282.

48. "This Program May Be Harmful to Your Child," *Saturday Review*, Oct. 9, 1971, p. 64.

49. *Cf.* John Merrill and Ralph Lowenstain, *Media, Messages, and Men; New Perspectives in Communications.* New York, David McKay, 1971, pp. 136-51.

50. James D. Halloran, "The Problems We Face," *Journal of Communication*, Winter 1975, p. 21. "Violence on T.V.—Does It Affect Our Society?" *T.V. Guide*, June 14, 1975.

51. *The Public's Attitude Toward Television and Other Media*, Report of a Study by Elmo Roper and Associates, New York, Television Information Office, 1962, p. 18.

52. "Polyps and Patriotism," *Newsweek*, July 13, 1964, p. 86.

53. Howard G. Garner, "An Adolescent Suicide, the Mass Media and the Educator," *Adolescence*, Summer 1975, pp. 241-45.

54. Bob Greene, "More Proof TV Violence Kills Kids," *Peoria Journal Star*, Sept. 18, 1977.

55. "Did TV Make Him Do It?" *Time*, October 10, 1977.

56. "Scientist Calls for Ban on TV, Movie Violence," *Chicago Tribune*, Oct. 16, 1977.

57. Victor B. Cline, "The Scientists vs. Pornography: An Untold Story," *Intellect*, May-June 1976, p. 574.

58. David Manning White, "Mass Culture in America; Another Point of View," in Bernard Rosenberg and David Manning White, *Mass Culture, The Popular Arts in America*, Glencoe, Ill.: Free Press, 1957, p. 13.

59. *The Freedom to Read*, Statement by the Westchester Conference of the American Library Association and the American Book Publishers Council, May 1953, proposition 7.

60. "FBI Chief Declares U.S. is 'Indulgent Toward Filth'," *Des Moines Sunday Register*, Dec. 17, 1963.

61. Curtis Bok, "If We are to Act Like Free Men," *Saturday Review*, Feb. 13, 1954, p. 9.

62. Cf. "College Papers Face Obscenity Charges, Censorship Threats," *Chronicle of Higher Education*, Dec. 9, 1968, p. 1.

63. Elihu Katz and Paul Lazarsfeld, *Personal Influence; the Part Played by People in the Flow of Mass Communications*, Glencoe, Free Press, 1955, pp. 32-33.

64. *Bulletin of the National Association for Better Radio and Television*, Nov. 1952, quoted by Edgar Dale, "Introduction" to 53rd Yearbook of the Society for the Study of Education, Chicago, University of Chicago Press, 1954, pt. 2, p. 2.

65. "Entertainment Without Violence," *Newsweek*, June 24, 1968, p. 26.

66. Alberta Siegel, "Communicating with the Next Generation." *Journal of Communication*, Autumn 1975, p. 23.

67. John C. Merrill and Ralph L. Lowenstein, *Media, Messages, and Men*, New York, McKay, 1971, pp. 125–132.

68. Ralph W. Emerson, "Self Reliance," *Essays*, Boston, Houghton Mifflin, 1883, p. 47.

69. A. L. Kroeber, *Anthropology*, New York, Harcourt, 1948, p. 9.

70. Ralph Linton, *The Tree of Culture*, New York, Knopf, 1955, p. 3.

71. William O. Stanley and others, *Social Foundations of Education*, New York, Dryden Press, 1956, p. 13.

72. George Murdock, "How Culture Changes," in Harry Shapiro, ed., *Man, Culture, and Society*, London, Oxford, 1971, p. 320.

73. Frank R. Leavis, *Education and the University*, New York, Stewart, 1948, p. 148.

74. Walt Whitman, "Democratic Vistas," in *Complete Poetry and Prose of Walt Whitman*, New York, Pellegrini, 1948, p. 234.

75. Arthur A. Berger, *Pop Culture*, Dayton, Ohio, Pilaum-Standard, n.d., p. 9.

76. Jesse Hine, "In Defense of Popular Culture in the Classroom," *English Journal*, Sept. 1972, p. 907.

77. Paul Lazarsfeld and Robert Merton, "Mass Communication, Popular Taste and Organized Social Action," in *The Communication of Ideas*, ed., by Lyman Bryson, New York, Harper, 1948, p. 118.

78. Patrick D. Hazard, "The Entertainer as Hero: a Problem of the Mass Media," *Journalism Quarterly*, Autumn 1962, p. 436.

79. Grayson Kirk, "The Three R's of Education Today," National Education Association 92nd Annual Meeting Proceedings, New York, 1954, pp. 43–4.

80. Lancelot Hogben, *Dangerous Thoughts*, New York, Norton, 1949, p. 216.

81. Robert M. Hutchins, "A Conversation on Education," *Library Journal*, Aug. 1963, p. 2825.

82. Paul L. MacKendrick, "Some Thoughts on Humanists and the Mass Media," *ACLS Newsletter*, Fall 1956, p. 3.

83. Rene Maheu, "The Intruders," *UNESCO Courier*, Feb. 1967, p. 23.

84. Francis C. Pray, "The Great Public Relations Mythology Trap and a Way Out," American College Public Relations Association 1961 National Conference, Denver, 1961, pp. 12, 14.

85. Gilbert Seldes, *The Public Arts*, New York, Simon and Schuster, 1956, p. 302.

86. Daymond Turner, "Humanities at the Barricades?" *South Atlantic Bulletin*, March 1957, p. 6.

87. Wilbur Schramm, "Mass Media and Educational Policy," in *60th Yearbook of the National Society for the Study of Education*, Chicago, University of Chicago Press, 1961, pt. 2, p. 229.

88. William D. Boutwell, ed., *Using Mass Media in the Schools*, New York, Appleton-Century-Crofts, 1962, p. 97.

Chapter 7: MEDIA POWER AND CAMPUS POWER IN STRIDE

1. Cf. Jay W. Stein, "Teaching and Learning in a World of Print," *Educational Forum*, May 1961, pp. 483–87.

2. Arthur Schlesinger. "Is Gutenberg Dead?" in K. J. McGarry, *Mass Communications; Selected Readings for Librarians*, Hamden, Conn., Linnet Books, 1972, p. 137.

3. Warren Ziegler, "Notes Toward a Social Philosophy for Adult Education," *Adult Leadership*, April 1976, pp. 255–56.

4. Alfred N. Whitehead, *The Aims of Education and Other Essays*, New York, Macmillan, 1929, p. 67.

5. Ernest O. Melby, "Human Relations in Education," in Proceedings of the National Conference on Human Relations Education, New York, 1955, p. 5.

6. William E. Hocking, *Experiment in Education*, Chicago, Regnery, 1954, p. 10.

7. Norman Foerster, *The American State University, Its Relation to Democracy*, Chapel Hill, University of North Carolina Press, 1937, p. 272.

8. Franklin Bobbitt, *How to Make a Curriculum*, Boston, 1924, p. 35.

9. St. Aurelius Augustine, "The Teacher," xiv, 45, in *Augustine: Earlier Writings.*, Philadelphia, Westminster, 1953, p. 100.

10. Seneca, *Epistolae*, cvi, p. 12.

11. William H. Hartley, "Records in the Social Studies," in *The Recording as a Teaching Tool*, ed. by Esther L. Berg and Florence B. Freedman, New York, Folkways Records, 1955, p. 8.

12. Southern University Conference, 1953, ed. by E. M. Gwathmey, Edgewater Park, Mississippi, 1953, pp. 40-42.

13. *The Daily Texan*, a student newspaper quoted in *College Management*, May 1, 1968, p. 6.

14. For the author's early version of media approach, see Jay W. Stein, "An Awareness Approach to Continuing Liberal-General Education," *Adult Education*, Spring 1964, pp. 142-45.

15. Martin McCullough, "A Multi-Media Approach to English," *English Journal*, October, 1968, p. 6.

16. Ann C. Heintz and others, *Mass Media; a Worktext in the Processes of Modern Communication*. Chicago, Loyola University Press, 1974, p. 4.

17. "Better Teaching Electrically," *Media Method*, February 1973, p. 12.

18. Lee A. Dubridge, "Science and Liberal Education," *Liberal Education*, May, 1964, p. 272.

19. William H. Kilpatrick, *Remaking the Curriculum*, New York, Newson, 1936, pp. 76, 87.

20. Benson R. Snyder, "The Invisible Curriculum," Panel discussion at 48th Annual Meeting of the American Council on Education, October 7, 1965, mimeo, pp. 1, 4.

21. Jay W. Stein, *How Society Governs Education*, Danville, Ill., Interstate, 1975, pp. 59, 64.

22. Paul Hartmann and Charles Husband, *Racism and the Mass Media; a Study of the Role of the Mass Media in the Formation of White Beliefs and Attitudes in Britain*, Totawa, N.J., Rowman and Litchfield, 1974.

23. "White on Black," *Newsweek*, March 11, 1968, p. 87.

Chapter 8: A MASSIVE CHALLENGE FOR TOMORROW

1. Lewis Mumford, *The Story of Utopias*, New York, Peter Smith, 1921, pp. 24-25.

2. David Riesman, *Individualism Reconsidered and Other Essays*, Glencoe, Free Press, 1954, p. 72.

3. Charles Frankel, "Piercing the Veil of the Commonplace," *Chronicle of Higher Education*, May 3, 1976, p. 32.

4. Wilbur Schramm, *Men, Messages and Media*. New York, Harper and Row, 1973, pp. 184, 188.

5. *The People of New York State and Today's Challenge to Education, a Call to Action by the Regents of the State of New York*, Albany, 1959, pp. 9-10.

6. John C. Daly, "The News Media: The Public Right to Know," *Vital Speeches*, April 15, 1968, pp. 407-10.

7. Carnegie Corporation of New York, *Annual Report*, 1956, p. 38.

8. See, among other accounts of pioneer endeavors, *Better Learning Through Current Materials*, ed. by Lucien Kinney and Katharine Dresden, Stanford, Stanford University Press, 1949, pp. 40-41; William R. Idol, "Language and Mass Media: A Tool and Its Application," *Clearing House*, Oct. 1963, pp. 121-22; Jay W. Stein, "An Assignment Worth Trying," *Social Studies*, Feb. 1966, pp. 58-66; *Using Mass Media in Teaching English*, Albany, New York State Education Department, 1960.

9. Jay W. Stein, "A Study of Two Cultural Forces," *College and University*, Spring 1965, pp. 301-06.

10. Harry J. Skornia, "The Impact of Radio and Television on Education in U.S.A.," in *Communication Media and the School*, Yearbook of Education, 1960, ed. by George Z. F. Bereday and Joseph A. Lauwerts, Tarrytown-on-Hudson, World Book, 1960, p. 159.

11. Robert C. O'Hara, *Media for the Millions; the Process of Mass Communication*, New York, Random House, 1961, p. ix.

12. Jack Behar and Ben Lieberman, "Paradise Regained or McLuhanacy?" *Teachers College Record*, April 1965, p. 647.

13. "The Critical Receiver Analyzing and Evaluating," in Robert C. O'Hara, *op. cit.*, ch. 18.

14. Kelvin B. Canavan, *Mass Media Education* (Curriculum Guidelines for Secondary Schools), Sydney, Catholic Education Office, 1975, p. 20.

15. Henry W. Brosin, "Information Theory and Clinical Medicine," in Brockway McMillan, *Current Trends in Information Theory*, Pittsburgh, University of Pittsburgh Press, 1953, p. 170.

16. James Russell Lowell, "A Fable for Critics," in *Complete Poetical Works*, Boston, Houghton Mifflin, 1924, p. 120.

17. William H. Kilpatrick, *Remaking the Curriculum*, New York, Newson, 1963, p. 44.

18. Rene Maheu, "The Intruders," *UNESCO Courier*, Feb. 1967, pp. 23-4.

19. Stanley E. Hyman,"Ideals, Dangers, and Limitations," in Norman Jacobs, ed., *Culture for the Millions?* Princeton, Van Nostrand, 1961, pp. 137-41.

20. Association for Higher Education, *Resolutions, 18th National Conference on Higher Education*, Chicago, 1963, p. 1.

21. Harold Taylor, *The University and Social Change*, Boston, Boston University Press, 1962, p. 14.

22. Joseph De France, ABC-TV, "Meet the Professor," December 2, 1962.

23. R. Freeman Butts, *The College Charts Its Course*, New York, McGraw Hill, 1939, p. 277.

24. Selen W. Barnett, "They Don't Hear The Music: The Plight and Possibility of Liberal Education," *Educational Record*, Spring 1968, p. 176.

25. Cf., L. R. Palmer, "Teamwork," *The Times Literary Supplement*, Feb. 6, 1964.

26. Morris L. Ernst, *Utopia 1976*, New York, Rinehart, 1955, p. 143.

27. Charles G. Wrenn and D. L. Harley, Time on Their Hands, *A Report on Leisure, Recreation and Young People*, Washington, American Council on Education, 1941, p. 35.

28. Thomas Guback, "Social Context and Creativity in Mass Communications," *Journal of Aesthetic Education*, Jan. 1974, pp. 63, 79-80.

29. Quoted in Robert P. Rosenthal and Lenore Jacobson, *Pygmalion in the Classroom*, New York, Holt, 1968, p. 183.

30. W. Macneile Dixon, *The Human Situation*, New York, Longmans, Green, 1937, p. 73.

31. "College by Newspaper," *Time*, Jan. 21, 1974, p. 53.

32. Henry S. Resnick, "Putting VD on Public TV," *Saturday Review*, Oct. 14, 1972, p. 33.

33. Joseph J. Schwab, *College Curriculum and Student Protest*, University of Chicago Press, 1969, p. 179.

34. Joseph Wood Krutch, "Is our Common Man Too Common?" *Saturday Review*, Jan. 10, 1953, p. 8.

35. William L. Rivers and Wilbur Schramm, *Responsibility in Mass Communication*, rev. ed., New York, Harper and Row, 1969, p. 250.

36. Ronald and Beatrice Gross, "A Nation of Learners," *American Education*, vol. 11, no. 2, 1975, p. 16-29.

37. For enthusiastic reference to the pleasure of learning see, for example, Francis H. Horn, "The Ends for Which We Educate," *Educational Forum*, Jan. 1964, p. 141; Gilbert Highet, *The Pleasures of Learning*, Commencement Address, Syracuse University, May 29, 1960; and Theodore Sizer, *Places for Learning, Places for Joy; Speculations on American School Reform*, Boston, Harvard University Press, 1973.

38. George Eliot, *Middlemarch* (1872) Bk, 3, ch. 29, New York, Collier, n.d., p. 128.

39. Hugh Duncan, *Communication and Social Order*, London, Oxford University Press, 1962, pp. 404-05.

40. Joanne Palmisano, Letter to the Editor, *Look*, Nov. 28, 1967, p. 16.

41. John Ohliger, *Listening Groups; Mass Media in Adult Education*, Boston, Center for the Study of Liberal Education for Adults at Boston University, 1967, p. 1.

42. "Charles Silberman on Alternatives to Crisis," *American Association of Colleges for Teacher Education, Bulletin*, March 1971, p. 8.

43. Ernest O. Melby, "Human Relations in Education," National Conference on Human Relations Education, Proceedings, New York, 1955, p. 4.

44. Maurice Fabre, *A History of Communications*, New York, Hawthorn, 1963, p. 104.

45. Kenneth Keniston, *"The Uncommitted; Alienated Youth in American Society,"* New York, Harcourt, 1965, p. 444.

46. William R. Harper, *The Trend in Higher Education*, Chicago, 1905, p. 27.

Chapter 9: SYMMETRY OF WISDOM WITHOUT END

1. Andre Fontaine, "The Mass Media — A Need for Greatness," The *Annals* of the American Academy of Political and Social Science, May 1967, p. 84.

2. William M. Jones, "The Necessary Vision," *Liberal Education*, May 1963, p. 290.

3. Thomas S. Eliot, "The Rock," in *Collected Poems*, 1909-35, New York, Harcourt, 1936, p. 179.

INDEX